P9-DTA-405

Better Homes and Gardens®

LOW-COST COOKING

© 1980 by Meredith Corporation, Des Moines, Iowa.
All Rights Reserved. Printed in the United States of America.
First Edition. First Printing.
Library of Congress Catalog Card Number: 79-53046
ISBN: 0-696-00541-7

BETTER HOMES AND GARDENS® BOOKS
Editor in Chief: James A. Autry
Editorial Director: Neil Kuehnl
Executive Art Director: William J. Yates

Editor: Gerald M. Knox
Art Director: Ernest Shelton
Associate Art Directors: Neoma Alt West, Randall Yontz
Copy and Production Editors: David Kirchner, Lamont Olson, David A. Walsh
Assistant Art Director: Harijs Priekulis
Senior Graphic Designer: Faith Berven
Graphic Designers: Linda Ford, Sheryl Veenschoten, Tom Wegner

Food Editor: Doris Eby
Senior Associate Food Editor: Sharyl Heiken
Senior Food Editors: Sandra Granseth, Elizabeth Woolever
Associate Food Editors: Mary Cunningham, Bonnie Lasater, Marcia Stanley, Joy Taylor, Pat Teberg
Recipe Development Editor: Marion Viall
Test Kitchen Director: Sharon Golbert
Test Kitchen Home Economists: Jean Brekke, Kay Cargill, Marilyn Cornelius, Maryellyn Krantz, Marge Steenson

Low-Cost Cooking
Editors: Mary Cunningham, Pat Teberg
Copy and Production Editor: David A. Walsh
Graphic Designer: Sheryl Veenschoten

On the cover:
Enticing entreès for the budget-conscious cook—clockwise from top left are zesty *Pork Chop and Pasta Dinner*, elegant *Chicken-Broccoli Crepes*, *Savory Scotch Meat Loaves*, and *Curried Fish Fillets*. (See index for recipe pages.)

Better Homes and Gardens
TEST KITCHEN®

Our seal assures you that every recipe in *Low-Cost Cooking* is endorsed by the Better Homes and Gardens Test Kitchen. Each recipe is tested for family appeal, practicality, and deliciousness.

Contents

Cutting Food Costs

"Every time I go to the store, my grocery bill goes up." People throughout the country are saying this almost daily, and more than likely you've said it, too. It's little wonder you feel this way. Food costs do keep rising. Sometimes, increases reflect the cost of seasonal foods, but the overall rise indicates a new, higher level of prices.

To complicate matters, large food markets offer more than 10,000 items that may tempt you to forget costs and to indulge in impulse buying.

The challenge is to keep spending within your specific budget without lowering the quality of food you buy. And that's what *Low-Cost Cooking* is all about. If "low-cost" conjures up thoughts of penny-pinching and dull routine, revise your thinking! "Low-cost" means staying within your budget, planning how you spend your money. You may ask "How do I plan?" Simple. Start with a realistic budget, then plan your menus and shopping around that budget.

Planning Menus

The best way to approach menu planning is to plan for several days or a week at a time. Gather together newspaper food ads, recipes, and information on the Basic Four Food Groups (see page 6).

When planning consider nutrition, family preferences, current good food buys, preparation time, food on hand, and available storage space. Although all this may take a little extra time each week, the financial savings more than pay for the added time you'll spend planning.

Here are some helpful guidelines for menu planning:

—Plan your menus around the main dish because the largest part of the food dollar is spent on meat.

—Use meat-stretching main dishes such as casseroles, soups, and stews. Occasionally substitute less-expensive items such as cooked dried legumes, eggs, and dairy products for meat. (For information on meat substitutes, see page 56.)

—Serve only 2-ounce portions of cooked meat. Many persons eat more than 4 to 6 ounces of meat daily. To figure out how much meat to buy to fulfill this 2-ounce serving, see the Meat Buying Price Chart on page 7.

—To divert the family's attention from smaller meat servings, concentrate on making the rest of the meal enticing. For example, plan a variety of side dish salads and vegetables, and try new homemade breads.

—Watch the newspaper ads closely. Plan some of your menus around specials. And don't read only the ads; newspaper food columnists often cover the food market and have tips on local bargains.

—The end of the month, when new food shipments arrive at food markets, usually is a good time for specials (especially on canned and frozen foods). Plan your menus with this in mind.

—Whenever you plan menus, consider the foods your family prefers. A menu or recipe isn't a money saver if your family won't eat the food and you end up discarding it.

—Sometimes savings must be considered in terms of time as well as money. Most convenience foods are not low-budget foods; the less preparation time you have available, the more money you will need to allow for timesaving foods. However, some convenience foods can cost you less than if you made the same thing from scratch. Some of the biggest bargains are frozen orange juice concentrate, bottled lemon juice, canned and frozen peas or green beans, cake and pudding mixes, and condensed canned soups. When your time is particularly short, add slightly more-expensive but still economical foods (such as frozen French-fried potatoes, refrigerated biscuits, and muffin mixes) to your purchases.

—Remember: It's the *total* cost that counts. Even a casserole is not a cost cutter when it calls for expensive ingredients.

Make a Shopping List

After you've planned your menus, make out a shopping list. A well-organized list is important when trying to maintain a budget. Use these suggestions for your list:

—Make out your shopping list from the menus and recipes you plan to prepare and serve.

—Put the advertised price and brand of sale items on your list.

—Use coupons with common sense. Buying things you don't need or are unlikely to use just because you have a coupon is not a bargain.

—Record the amount of food you need to buy; consult recipes and the Meat Buying Price Chart on page 7.

—Organize your list so items are grouped as they appear in the grocery store. That way you won't be tempted a second time to buy things that aren't on your list (and you'll save shopping time).

Shopping

With your shopping list, you're on your way to successful budgeting. But you must also be a wise shopper to achieve savings.

Sticking to your list is a good general rule to follow, but keep your eyes open for unadvertised store specials that are genuine bargains.

(Make sure you're not just saving a few pennies on an item that was overpriced to begin with.) Learn to identify a loss leader—an item the store takes a loss on in the hopes that you'll do more shopping for things not necessarily on sale. Also, take advantage of low prices on seasonal items such as fruits and vegetables (see the chart on page 96), and items sold at lower prices during high periods of normal production cycles, such as eggs. Here are a few other tips to help control spending at the store:

—Compare prices of fresh, frozen, and canned fruits and vegetables based on the cost *per serving*. Usually, but not always, canned goods are less expensive than their frozen or fresh counterparts.

—Choose the grade and quality of canned goods that fit your use. When shape, uniformity of size, and color are not important, use the thriftiest form; you get equally good flavor and nutritive value.

—Check out prices on store and generic (or no-name) brands versus national brands. If they meet your quality needs, you can save money by using them.

—Read labels carefully, picking out the form, grade, and ingredient listing, as well as the price and net weight.

—Don't shop when you're hungry. Food looks especially enticing when you have an empty stomach, and you may find yourself buying more food than planned.

—Buy fresh produce that looks fresh and is in good condition. It's a waste of time and money if you have to cut away bad spots and throw away poor quality food.

—Select foods that are packaged simply. Fancy or superfluous packaging is generally more costly.

—Be aware that more expensive items are sometimes placed on shelves at eye level and that less expensive ones are where you have to reach or stoop for them.

—Choose large packages of staple foods instead of small ones if you use the product often or in large quantities. Shop for the largest size you can store easily.

—If you have freezer space, purchase specials in large quantities, but turn over the freezer supply at least once a year.

—Buy nonfat dry milk powder for cooking and drinking. If you want a richer product for drinking, mix equal parts of fluid whole milk and reconstituted nonfat dry milk

—Use evaporated milk in cooking, too. To substitute it for regular fluid milk, combine equal portions of evaporated milk and water.

—Milk by the gallon usually costs less per serving than milk by the half gallon or quart. Large sizes of nonfat dry milk powder cost less per serving than small sizes, also.

—Purchase dairy products from the grocery store because a home delivery service usually ups the price considerably.

—Cut down on luxury foods such as snack items, soft drinks, convenience items, and ready-to-eat bakery products.

—Margarine in a tub costs more than stick margarine, but both cost less than butter. If you do buy butter, buy it in bulk and quarter it yourself.

—Make as few trips to the store as possible. Each trip means money spent for gas and another opportunity to buy unnecessary items that you see.

Preparation and Storage

Proper preparation and storage of food once it is purchased is important. Careful planning and shopping are useless if your handling and storage techniques are poor. Take groceries straight home, unpack them, and immediately store them under the proper conditions.

Use perishable foods during their peak of quality, so there will be little, if any, to throw away. Use all edible parts of foods. For example, remove only thin layers of peel from fruits or vegetables, and carefully separate edible from inedible portions.

Here are some guidelines for storing specific foods.

Eggs: Refrigerate in the original container or in a covered container with small end of eggs down. Cover leftover egg yolks with cold water and refrigerate in a tightly covered container; use within 2 days. Leftover egg whites will keep for up to 10 days if refrigerated in a tightly covered container.

Dairy products: Tightly cover cottage cheese, hard and soft cheeses, milk, and butter or margarine; refrigerate. Use cottage cheese within 5 days and soft cheeses within 2 weeks. Hard cheeses, when tightly wrapped, will keep several months. A good rule of thumb is: The softer the cheese, the more perishable it is. Place strong-flavored cheeses in tightly covered jars in the refrigerator so the odor and flavor won't permeate other foods. Refrigerate process cheese spreads once the package is opened. Tightly wrapped, process cheese spreads will keep in the refrigerator several months.

Hard cheese and process cheese spread can be frozen for longer storage. Tightly wrap in moisture-vaporproof material; freeze. Use hard cheese within 6 weeks. Process cheese spread can be frozen up to 4 months.

Fresh fruit: Remove injured fruit; use promptly or discard. Ripen tomatoes, melons, peaches, pears, and plums at room temperature and out of direct sunlight; then refrigerate. Store bananas and uncut pineapple in a cool place. Refrigerate other fruit.

When fruit is covered or in plastic bag, ensure there are holes for air circulation. Remember: Fruits have a fairly short storage life; store only a few days to 2 weeks.

Cutting Food Costs (continued)

Fresh vegetables: Store potatoes, onions, and winter squash in a cool, dry place. Clean when ready to use. Wash, drain, and dry greens, cabbage, carrots, celery, radishes, and green onions. Wrap separately in moisture-vaporproof bags; refrigerate. Refrigerate other vegetables; clean before using.

Meats, poultry, fish: Fresh meat or poultry, paper wrapped from the butcher, should be rewrapped loosely in waxed paper or clear plastic wrap before refrigerating. Tightly rewrap fresh fish in moisture-vaporproof material before refrigerating. You can refrigerate prepackaged meat, poultry, or fish as is. Refrigerator storage guidelines are:

Beef	2 to 4 days
Fresh pork	2 to 4 days
Ham and smoked pork shoulder arm picnic	1 week
Other smoked pork	3 to 4 days
Whole poultry	2 to 3 days
Cut up poultry	1 to 2 days
Fish	1 to 2 days
Sausage and frankfurters	4 to 5 days
Variety meats	1 to 2 days
Cooked meats	4 to 5 days
Cooked poultry	1 to 2 days
Luncheon meats	1 week

To keep meat, poultry, or fish longer, tightly wrap in moisture-vaporproof material; freeze. Recommended freezer times are:

Cooked meats	3 to 4 months
Ground meats	3 to 4 months
Beef	6 to 12 months
Fresh pork	3 to 6 months
Smoked pork	2 months
Fish	6 to 9 months
Variety meats	3 to 4 months
Cooked poultry	1 month
Luncheon meats	Don't freeze

Canned foods: Store in a cool, dry place. After you open a canned food, cover the can and store in the refrigerator.

Flours, cereals: Store at room temperature in tightly covered containers.

Basic Four Food Groups

For nutritious meals your family deserves, select foods each day from the Basic Four Food Groups.

Fruit and Vegetable Group: Four or more servings should be eaten daily to provide vitamins A and C and other nutrients. Include one serving (½ cup) of a good source of vitamin C (grapefruit, oranges, broccoli, cantaloupe, or fresh strawberries) or two fair sources (cabbage, potatoes, spinach, tangerines, or tomatoes) daily. Every other day serve one good source of vitamin A (broccoli, cantaloupe, carrots, dark green leaves, sweet potatoes, or winter squash).

Milk Group: Milk is the primary source of calcium, and also provides riboflavin, protein, phosphorous, and vitamins A and D. Children younger than 12 should drink 2 to 3 cups daily; children 12 and older, 3 to 4 cups; and adults, 2 cups. Suitable equivalents for *1 cup* of milk are: 1½ ounces cheddar or American cheese or process cheese spread; 2 cups cottage cheese; 1 cup yogurt; or 1¾ cups ice cream.

Meat Group: Beef, veal, lamb, pork, poultry, fish and seafood, eggs, legumes, nuts, and peanut butter are in this group. These foods provide iron, thiamin, niacin, riboflavin, and other nutrients. Eat two 2- to 3-ounce servings of cooked meat, poultry, or fish daily. See page 56 for serving sizes of the other foods.

Grain Group: Breads, cereals, cornmeal, crackers, flour, grits, pastas, rice, and baked products make up this group. Buy whole grain or enriched products; they are good sources of thiamin, niacin, riboflavin, and other nutrients. Offer four or more servings daily (one serving is 1 slice of bread or ½ cup cooked cereal, pasta, or rice).

Comparing Meat Costs

Find the best meat buys by learning to use the Meat Buying Price Chart (opposite). This table helps you compare the cost *per serving* of meats. The servings listed are based on approximately 2 ounces of cooked meat each. Since the chart is designed to help you stretch meat, portions may be smaller than you are accustomed to serving. A 2-ounce serving size, however, gives maximum savings on meat with good nutrition in mind. These guidelines are used throughout recipes in this book.

The meats listed in the chart are divided into three groups. The first group consists of boneless cuts, those that have very little fat, and canned meats or fish. Some differences exist in shrinkage and cooking loss among members of this group. For the most part, however, plan on six servings to the pound.

The second group is made up of meat cuts with small bones and boneless cuts that have a moderate amount of fat. Fresh or frozen fish and seafood are also a part of this group. Figure four servings per pound.

The final group comprises meats with a high proportion of bone, as well as cuts that are extremely fatty. These cuts do not stretch far, so plan on only two servings per pound.

Here's how the chart works. Find the price per pound in the left-hand column. Run your finger *across* this row to the column that includes the specific meat you're pricing. For example, you'll find ground beef at $1.69 a pound is $.42 a serving, but country-style ribs at $1.39 a pound works out to $.70 a serving. The chart tells you that even though ground beef costs more *per pound,* it costs less *per serving* than country-style ribs.

Meat Buying Price Chart

Price per Pound	Cost per Serving of Boneless and Lean Meat (6 servings per pound)	Cost per Serving of Meat with Some Bone or Fat (4 servings per pound)	Cost per Serving of Meat with Much Bone or Fat (2 servings per pound)
$ .49	$ .08	$ .12	$ .25
.59	.10	.15	.30
.69	.12	.17	.35
.79	.13	.20	.40
.89	.15	.22	.45
.99	.16	.25	.50
1.09	.18	.27	.55
1.19	.20	.30	.60
1.29	.22	.32	.65
1.39	.23	.35	.70
1.49	.25	.37	.75
1.59	.26	.40	.80
1.69	.28	.42	.85
1.79	.30	.45	.90
1.89	.32	.47	.95
1.99	.33	.50	1.00
2.09	.35	.52	1.05
2.19	.36	.55	1.10
2.29	.38	.57	1.15
2.39	.40	.60	1.20
2.49	.42	.62	1.25
2.59	.43	.65	1.30
2.69	.45	.67	1.35
2.79	.46	.70	1.40
2.89	.48	.72	1.45
	Boneless Beef and Pork Roast, Beef Flank Steak, Boneless Ham, Stew Meat, Liver, Heart, Tongue, Canadian-Style Bacon, Frankfurters and Sausage, Bologna, Other Luncheon Meat, Canned Fish and Seafood	Round Steak, Beef Chuck Pot Roast, Smoked Pork Shoulder Arm Picnic, Pork Blade and Arm Steaks, Ham with Bone in, Ground Meat, Bulk Pork Sausage, Fresh or Frozen Fish and Seafood, Lamb, Pork Chops, Beef/Pork Cubed Steaks	Poultry, Pork Spareribs, Country-Style Ribs, Beef Short Ribs, Lamb Shanks, Ham Shanks, and Oxtail

Money-Saving Menus

A meatless meal (such as the one below) needs careful planning to make sure it is nutritionally balanced. Of special concern is an adequate amount of high-quality protein. Also important, as in all meal planning, is to make the meal attractive and tasty.

Dairy products are the main protein source in this main dish. Drinking a glass of milk with the meal helps satisfy your protein requirements and assures adequate calcium, too. Various fruits and grain products round out the meal.

Plan a meatless meal around the main dish. Because Cheesy Broccoli Bake is a mixture of foods, serve some accompaniments that are "whole"—such as breadsticks or crackers and cupcakes or cake. A meal can look too "busy" if every dish served is a mixture.

Since Cheesy Broccoli Bake is a soft-textured baked dish, a frozen salad is an ideal accompaniment. A fruit-filled gelatin salad would also provide temperature and some texture contrast. Breadsticks add needed crunch to the main course.

For dessert, serve either Peanut Butter Cupcakes or Carrot-Banana Cake. Both introduce additional flavor, color, and nutrients into the meal.

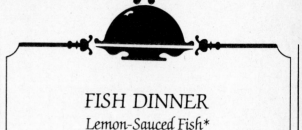

MEATLESS DINNER SPECIAL

*Cheesy Broccoli Bake**
*Fruit Cocktail Freeze**
or
*Salad Ambrosia**
Crisp Breadsticks or Crackers*
*Peanut Butter Cupcakes**
or
*Carrot-Banana Cake**
Coffee or Tea Milk

FISH DINNER

*Lemon-Sauced Fish**
or
*Fillets Parmesan**
Buttered Brussels Sprouts
*Fruit Medley with Pineapple Dressing**
*French Bread**
Margarine or Butter
*Pumpkin Dessert Soufflé**
Coffee or Tea Milk

Well-planned menus have eye and taste appeal in addition to being within your budget of money, time, and energy. Variety in color, form of the food, flavor, texture, and temperature are important parts in the art of planning a good meal.

This fish dinner (above) is an example of a well-planned meal. Besides being nutritionally sound, it appeals visually. The colors of the foods are different but do not clash, and the sizes and shapes of the foods offer variety (square fish fillets, round brussels sprouts, sliced fruits, soufflé mounded in a round serving dish). Be careful to avoid having too many dishes that are mixtures, too many small pieces, or too many similar shapes in a meal.

This menu has taste appeal, too. Many textures are included—the delicate textures of fish and fruit are complemented by the firmness of brussels sprouts, the chewiness of French bread, and the lightness of a soufflé. The flavors vary and complement one another. The delicate flavor of fish, the buttered vegetable, sweet salad, and spicy dessert go well together. Some foods are served hot (fish, brussels sprouts, coffee or tea) and others are cold (fruit medley, pumpkin soufflé, and milk).

*Recipes are in this book. See index for pages.

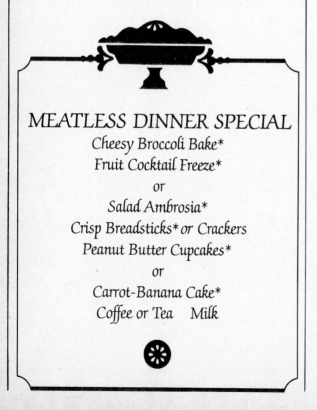

This hearty winter menu (below) is a winner. The protein from turkey meat is boosted by the addition of navy beans to the soup. The meal is well-balanced nutritionally, as it contains foods from all of the Basic Four Food Groups. It is pleasing to look at, too. Turkey, navy beans, carrots, celery, and turnips add color variety to the soup. More color and shape are added to the menu with your choice of vegetable relishes. The lime gelatin salad is topped with a lemon-yellow layer, and the cheese bread has a warm golden color. For dessert, serve rosy Apple-Cranberry Crisp or chocolate Easy Snack Cake. Notice that sizes, shapes, and colors contrast without clashing with each other.

The foods in this menu taste good together, too. The soft texture of the beans in the hot soup is contrasted by cold, crisp vegetable relishes. The gelatin salad adds a cool, light note to the meal, and homemade bread gives you something to sink your teeth into. The tartness of warm Apple-Cranberry Crisp with its crunchy topping or fine-textured Easy Snack Cake ends the meal nicely. You've also included a variety of temperatures: a hot soup, cold relishes and salad, and a warm dessert.

HEARTY SOUP SUPPER

Turkey Frame-Bean Soup*
Assorted Vegetable Relishes
Citrus Yogurt Squares*
Cheese Bread*
Margarine or Butter
Apple-Cranberry Crisp*
or
Easy Snack Cake*
Coffee or Tea Milk

SMOKED PORK SPECIAL

Barbecue-Sauced Shoulder Arm Picnic*
Cheese Scalloped Corn*
24-Hour Cabbage Salad*
Whole Wheat and Bran Rolls*
Margarine or Butter
Easy Orange Sherbet*
and
Oatmeal Crinkle Cookies*
Coffee or Tea Milk

This meal (above) is planned around a smoked pork shoulder arm picnic. By planning interesting side dishes such as those listed, you can serve smaller portions of meat, and end up with enough leftover pork shoulder arm picnic for another meal. Or, this would be a good meal to feed a crowd.

This food combination is as pleasing to look at as it is to eat. The pink color of the smoked meat is complemented by the golden color of Cheese Scalloped Corn and the sprightly green color of 24-Hour Cabbage Salad. Whole Wheat and Bran Rolls introduce a golden brown color and rounded shape. For dessert, Easy Orange Sherbet and Oatmeal Crinkle Cookies add additional variety in color and shape.

You'll please everyone's palate with this meal, too. Spicy barbecue-sauced meat is soothed by the creamy, cheese-flavored corn casserole. The crisp cabbage salad's sweet-sour dressing complements both the meat and vegetable, and homemade Whole Wheat and Bran Rolls add a mild nutlike flavor. Smooth sherbet is a cool and refreshing way to end this meal, with oatmeal cookies to accompany it. There is a pleasant balance of color, shape, texture, flavor, and temperatures in this meal.

*Recipes are in this book. See index for pages.

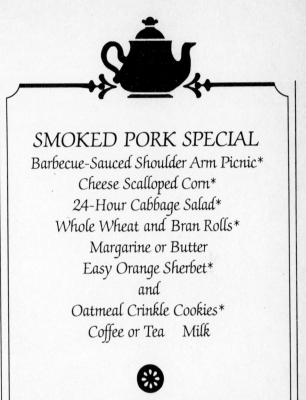

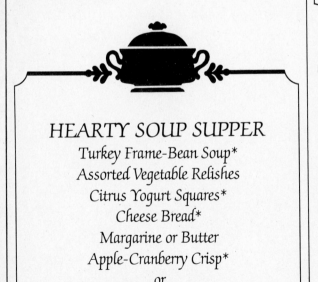

Main Dishes

This selection of economical main dishes is (clockwise from back left) *Chicken with Pineapple, Cheesy Stuffed Peppers, Fish Sticks Polynesian, Main Dish Pasta Ring,* and *Oriental Pot Roast.* (See index for recipe pages.)

Beef

arm roast

Economical beef cuts are more varied and flavorful than you may realize. As a cost-conscious shopper, you can find them at any meat counter, and, with a little know-how, create delicious, thrifty entrées.

Beef cuts vary in price according to the tenderness and popularity of the cut. Bargain-priced cuts are less tender than expensive loin and rib cuts, but taste every bit as good after long, slow cooking.

Economical Beef Cuts

Good beef buys include the shoulder cuts, the beef chuck *arm, 7-bone,* and *flat blade* pot roasts and steaks (see illustrations, below). These cuts need to be cooked using moist heat, such as braising or stewing. Plan on about 3 servings per pound.

An *arm roast* can save kitchen time—as well as money—if you buy one large roast (5 to 6 pounds) and cut it into sections (see illustration, above) for 3 meals as follows:

—Prepare steaks from section 1 in recipes calling for round steak.

—Use section 2 for pot roasts (beef cooked in liquid).

—Cube the meat in section 3 and use it in soups and stews.

The familiar *round steak* is lean and has little waste. A bonus is that a whole round steak can be divided into meat for several meals. This cut has 3 obvious sections that may be sold separately but at a much higher price per pound than the whole round steak; so it is worth your time and money to separate them yourself (see illustration, right).

—The eye of round (section 1) is the smallest muscle of the round. Either braise it or pot roast and thinly slice it for serving.

—The bottom round (section 2) requires long, slow cooking in liquid.

—The top round (section 3) is the largest and tenderest section of the round steak. Broil it to rare or medium doneness and slice thinly for serving.

Ground beef is still a good buy in spite of its rising prices.

To get more from your ground beef dollar, remember these tips:

—Oftentimes ground beef costs less per pound when you buy it in large quantities.

—Plan on 4 or 5 servings per pound of ground beef.

—The higher the fat content, the lower the price per pound. From highest fat content to lowest are hamburger, ground beef, ground chuck, and ground round.

—Because of the difference in fat

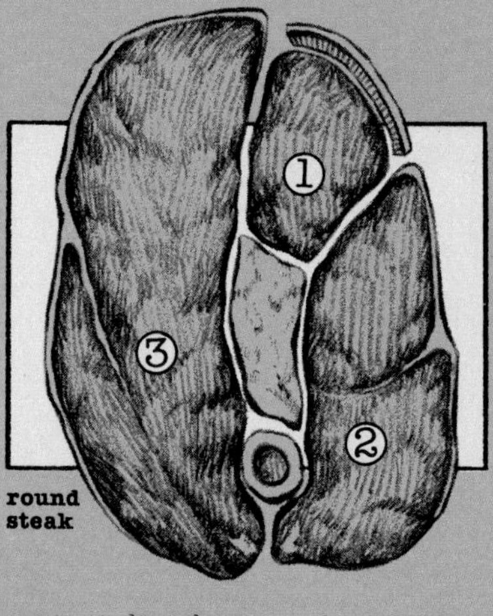

round steak

content, hamburger when cooked usually shrinks more than ground beef; that's why it costs less.

—Because their shrinkage is relatively high and they use a less tender meat, hamburger and ground beef are best suited for casseroles, skillets, soups, and similar dishes that include other ingredients. Your leaner grades of ground meat come from more popular cuts and may be less juicy.

—Save leftovers—even the bones—to make tasty stocks, soups, and stews. Leftover cooked meats are put to good use in casseroles, meat pies, salads, sandwiches, stuffed vegetables, and even pizzas. (See Index for recipes calling for leftover meats.)

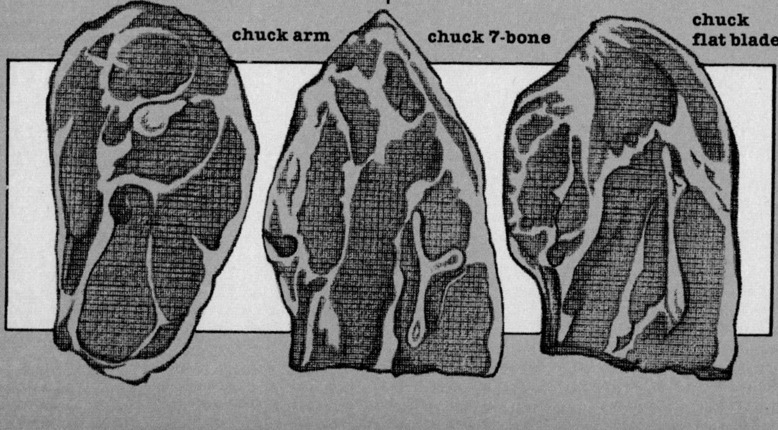

chuck arm

chuck 7-bone

chuck flat blade

Herbed Pot Roast Supreme

Sour cream and mushrooms add elegance to this seasoned pot roast—

- 2 slices bacon
- 1 2- to 3-pound beef chuck pot roast
- 1 10½-ounce can condensed beef broth
- ½ cup chopped onion
- 1 bay leaf
- 1 teaspoon worcestershire sauce
- ½ teaspoon dried thyme, crushed
- ¼ teaspoon salt
- ⅛ teaspoon pepper
- ½ cup dairy sour cream
- 2 tablespoons all-purpose flour
- 1 4-ounce can mushroom stems and pieces, drained
- 2 tablespoons snipped parsley
- Hot cooked noodles

In Dutch oven cook bacon till crisp. Drain, reserving drippings. Crumble bacon; set aside.

Trim excess fat from meat. Brown meat on all sides in reserved bacon drippings. Add beef broth, chopped onion, bay leaf, worcestershire sauce, thyme, salt, and pepper. Cover; simmer for 1½ to 2 hours or till meat is tender.

Remove meat to heated platter; keep warm. For sour cream sauce, skim fat from pan juices; discard bay leaf. Blend sour cream with flour. Stir about ¼ *cup* of the pan juices into sour cream mixture; return all to pan. Cook and stir till thickened; *do not boil.* Stir in mushrooms, snipped parsley, and crumbled bacon. Serve sour cream sauce with roast and hot cooked noodles. Makes 8 to 12 servings.

Mexican-Style Pot Roast

A spicy bite of chili peppers makes this an interesting pot roast variation—

- 1 3- to 3½-pound beef chuck pot roast *or* pork shoulder blade Boston roast
- 2 tablespoons cooking oil *or* shortening
- 1 7½-ounce can tomatoes, cut up
- 1 4-ounce can green chilies, drained, seeded, and chopped
- ¼ cup water
- ½ envelope (2 tablespoons) taco seasoning mix
- 2 teaspoons instant beef bouillon granules
- 1 teaspoon sugar
- ¼ cup cold water
- 2 tablespoons all-purpose flour
- Corn bread (optional)

Trim excess fat from beef or pork roast. In Dutch oven brown meat on both sides in hot oil or shortening. Combine *undrained* tomatoes, chopped green chilies, ¼ cup water, dry taco seasoning mix, beef bouillon granules, and sugar; pour over meat. Cover and simmer for 2 to 2½ hours or till meat is tender.

Remove meat to heated platter; keep warm. For gravy, pour pan juices into measuring cup. Skim off fat. Add water if necessary to make 1¾ cups liquid; transfer to saucepan. Blend the ¼ cup cold water into the flour; add to mixture in saucepan. Cook and stir till thickened and bubbly.

Slice meat; pass gravy. Serve with corn bread, if desired. Makes 10 to 12 servings.

Orange and Spice Pot Roast

- 1 3½- to 4-pound beef chuck pot roast, cut 1½ inches thick
- 2 tablespoons lemon juice
- 1 teaspoon salt
- 3 slices bacon
- 1 7½-ounce can tomatoes, cut up
- 1 cup orange juice
- ⅔ cup chopped onion
- ¼ cup snipped parsley
- 1 small bay leaf
- 1 clove garlic, minced
- 4 whole cloves
- 1 teaspoon sugar
- ½ teaspoon ground cinnamon
- ¼ cup cold water
- 2 tablespoons all-purpose flour
- Orange slices (optional)
- Snipped parsley (optional)

Trim excess fat from meat. Sprinkle meat with lemon juice and salt. In a large oven-going skillet cook bacon till crisp. Drain, reserving drippings. Crumble bacon and set aside.

Brown meat on all sides in reserved bacon drippings. Combine *undrained* tomatoes, orange juice, chopped onion, parsley, bay leaf, minced garlic, cloves, sugar, cinnamon, and cooked bacon; pour over meat. Cover and bake in 325° oven for 2 to 2½ hours or till meat is tender. Remove meat and vegetables to heated platter; keep warm. Remove bay leaf and discard.

To make gravy, skim fat from pan juices. Blend cold water into flour; stir into pan juices. Cook and stir till thickened and bubbly.

Garnish meat with orange slices and snipped parsley, if desired. Pass gravy with meat. Makes 12 to 16 servings.

Old-Fashioned Roast Dinner

1 3- to 4-pound beef chuck pot roast
2 tablespoons all-purpose flour
1 teaspoon salt
1/2 teaspoon dried marjoram, crushed
1/2 teaspoon dried thyme, crushed
1/4 teaspoon dried basil, crushed
1/4 teaspoon pepper
8 medium carrots, halved crosswise
4 medium onions, cut into wedges
1 pound small whole potatoes, peeled
2 tablespoons all-purpose flour
Snipped parsley

Trim excess fat from meat. In Dutch oven heat trimmings till 1 tablespoon fat accumulates; discard trimmings. Rub meat with 2 tablespoons flour. Brown meat in the hot fat. Sprinkle the 1 teaspoon salt, the marjoram, thyme, basil, and pepper over meat. Remove from heat; add 1 1/2 cups *water*. Cover; bake in 350° oven for 1 to 1 1/2 hours. Add carrots, onions, and potatoes; sprinkle with 1/2 teaspoon *salt*. Cover; return to oven and bake about 45 minutes more or till meat and vegetables are tender. Remove meat and vegetables to heated platter; keep warm.

Skim fat from pan juices. Add enough water to juices to make 1 1/2 cups liquid. Combine 1/2 cup cold *water* and 2 tablespoons flour; stir into pan juices. Cook and stir till thickened and bubbly. Cook 1 to 2 minutes more, stirring occasionally. Pour some of the gravy over meat. Pass remaining gravy. Garnish with snipped parsley. Makes 12 to 16 servings.

Pot Roast Italiano

Serve your favorite hot cooked pasta with this Italian-inspired roast—

1 3- to 4-pound beef chuck pot roast
2 tablespoons cooking oil *or* shortening
1 16-ounce can tomatoes, cut up
1 10 1/2-ounce can condensed beef broth
1 8-ounce can tomato sauce
2 cloves garlic, minced
1 teaspoon sugar
3/4 teaspoon dried oregano, crushed
3/4 teaspoon dried basil, crushed
1/8 teaspoon pepper
1/2 cup chopped green pepper
1/3 cup chopped onion
1/4 cup cold water
1/4 cup cornstarch
Hot cooked spaghetti *or* other pasta

Trim excess fat from meat. In Dutch oven brown meat on all sides in hot oil or shortening. Add *undrained* tomatoes, beef broth, tomato sauce, garlic, sugar, oregano, basil, and pepper. Cover and simmer for 1 1/2 hours. Add chopped green pepper and onion. Cover and simmer about 30 minutes more or till meat is tender.

Transfer roast to heated platter; keep warm. For sauce, skim excess fat from pan juices. Measure 4 cups juices (add water, if necessary). Blend together the cold water and cornstarch; stir into pan juices. Cook and stir till sauce is thickened and bubbly. Season sauce to taste with salt and pepper. Pass sauce with roast and hot cooked spaghetti. Makes 12 to 16 servings.

Oriental Pot Roast

Oriental seasonings penetrate this roast, pictured on pages 10 and 11—

1 2- to 3-pound beef chuck pot roast
1/3 cup cooking oil
1/3 cup soy sauce
2 tablespoons lemon juice
2 tablespoons honey
1 clove garlic, minced
1 1/4 teaspoons ground ginger
2 cups celery bias sliced into 1/2-inch pieces
4 medium carrots, bias sliced into 1/2-inch pieces (1 1/2 cups)
2 medium onions, quartered
1/4 cup cold water
1 tablespoon cornstarch

Trim excess fat from meat. Place meat in plastic bag; set in deep bowl. For marinade, combine cooking oil, soy sauce, lemon juice, honey, garlic, and ginger. Pour over meat; close bag. Marinate overnight in refrigerator; turn bag occasionally to distribute marinade.

Next day, transfer roast and marinade from bag to 4-quart Dutch oven. Cover; simmer for 1 hour. Add celery, carrots, and onions. Cover and simmer about 45 minutes more or till meat and vegetables are tender. Remove meat and vegetables to a heated platter; keep warm.

For gravy, skim excess fat from pan juices. Pour juices into 2-cup measure. Add water to juices if necessary to make 1 1/4 cups liquid; return to Dutch oven. Combine the 1/4 cup cold water and cornstarch; add to pan juices. Cook and stir till thickened and bubbly. Serve gravy with meat and vegetables. Makes 8 to 12 servings.

Sauerbraten-Style Pot Roast

The spiciness of this roast is enhanced by a surprise ingredient: grape jelly—

- 1 3- to 3½-pound beef chuck pot roast
- 2 tablespoons cooking oil *or* shortening
- 2 teaspoons salt
- ¼ teaspoon pepper
- 3 medium onions, sliced (1½ cups)
- ½ cup vinegar
- ⅓ cup water
- ⅓ cup grape jelly
- 2 bay leaves
- 1 teaspoon ground ginger
- ¼ cup all-purpose flour
- Hot buttered noodles
- Poppy seed (optional)

Trim excess fat from meat. In Dutch oven brown meat on all sides in cooking oil or shortening. Remove from heat; season with the salt and pepper. Top with onion. Combine vinegar, water, grape jelly, bay leaves, and ginger; pour over meat. Cover; simmer about 2½ hours or till meat is tender. Remove meat and onions to heated platter; keep warm. Remove and discard bay leaves.

For gravy, pour pan juices into large measuring cup; skim off excess fat, reserving ¼ cup fat. Add water to juices, if necessary, to make 2 cups liquid. Return reserved fat to Dutch oven; blend in flour. Add pan juices all at once; blend well. Cook and stir till thickened and bubbly; cook and stir 2 to 3 minutes more. Season gravy to taste with salt and pepper. Toss noodles with some poppy seed, if desired. Serve meat and gravy with hot buttered noodles. Makes 12 to 14 servings.

Easy Roast in Foil

- 1 2- to 3-pound beef chuck pot roast
- 1 10¾-ounce can condensed cream of mushroom soup
- ½ package (¼ cup) *regular* onion soup mix
- 4 medium potatoes, peeled and quartered
- 4 medium carrots, quartered crosswise

Trim excess fat from meat. Line shallow roasting pan with foil. Place meat in pan. Combine mushroom soup and dry onion soup mix; spread over roast. Cover; seal with foil. Bake in 325° oven 1 hour. Arrange potatoes and carrots around roast. Cover; continue baking about 45 minutes or till meat and vegetables are tender. Season to taste. Serves 8 to 12.

Mock Steak Diane

- 1 pound beef round steak, cut ½ to ¾ inch thick
- 2 tablespoons cooking oil
- 1 small onion, sliced and separated into rings
- 2 tablespoons margarine
- 1 4-ounce can mushroom stems and pieces, drained
- 1 tablespoon lemon juice
- 1 teaspoon dry mustard
- ½ teaspoon worcestershire sauce

Cut meat into 4 serving-size pieces; pound to ¼-inch thickness. Cook meat, 2 pieces at a time, in hot oil for 2 minutes. Turn; cook 2 minutes more. Remove to warm platter. Cook onion in margarine till just tender; add mushrooms, lemon juice, mustard, worcestershire, ½ teaspoon *salt*, and dash *pepper*; heat through. Spoon over steaks; sprinkle with snipped parsley, if desired. Serves 4.

Bacon-Wrapped Beef Kabobs

You'll be surprised how juicy and tender round steak is on these kabobs—

- 2 medium onions
- 2 medium green peppers, seeded and cut into 1½-inch squares
- 1 pound beef round steak, cut ½- to ¾-inch thick
- ½ teaspoon instant unseasoned meat tenderizer
- 6 to 8 slices bacon, halved crosswise
- 1 8¼-ounce can pineapple chunks
- ½ cup bottled barbecue sauce
- 2 tablespoons lemon juice
- Hot cooked rice (optional)

Parboil onions in boiling water, covered, for 5 minutes, adding green pepper squares last 2 minutes of cooking. Drain. Cool onions slightly; cut into wedges.

Thoroughly moisten round steak with water. Sprinkle instant meat tenderizer evenly over entire surface of meat. To ensure penetration and retain meat juices, pierce deeply with a fork at about ½ inch intervals. Cut meat into 1½-inch pieces.

Partially cook bacon; drain on absorbent paper toweling. Wrap half slices of bacon around each beef chunk; secure with wooden picks. Thread wrapped beef, onion wedges, green pepper squares, and pineapple chunks alternately on six 12-inch skewers.

Combine bottled barbecue sauce and lemon juice. Grill kabobs over *medium-hot* coals 12 to 15 minutes or till done, turning and basting often with barbecue sauce mixture. Serve with hot cooked rice, if desired. Makes 6 servings.

Spinach Beef Roll

- 2 tablespoons all-purpose flour
- 1/4 teaspoon garlic salt
- 1/8 teaspoon pepper
- 1 2-pound beef round steak, cut 3/4 inch thick
- 3/4 cup soft bread crumbs (1 slice)
- 1/2 of a 10-ounce package frozen chopped spinach, cooked and well drained (1/2 cup)
- 1/3 cup grated parmesan cheese
- 2 tablespoons finely chopped onion
- 1/4 teaspoon ground sage
- 2 tablespoons cooking oil *or* shortening
- 1 teaspoon instant beef bouillon granules
- 2/3 cup boiling water
- Hot cooked noodles (optional)

Combine flour, garlic salt, and pepper; pound into round steak till meat is about 1/4 inch thick. Cut meat in half lengthwise. Combine bread crumbs, drained spinach, parmesan cheese, chopped onion, and sage; spread spinach mixture over both pieces of meat. Roll up each piece jelly-roll style, starting from short side. Skewer or tie securely.

In skillet brown meat rolls slowly on all sides in hot cooking oil or shortening. Transfer to 10x6x2-inch baking dish. Dissolve beef bouillon granules in boiling water; pour over meat. Cover and bake in 350° oven for 35 minutes. Uncover; bake 15 to 25 minutes more or till meat is tender, basting occasionally with pan juices. To serve, remove skewers or string from meat rolls; slice meat rolls. Serve with hot cooked noodles, if desired. Pass pan juices with meat. Makes 8 servings.

Oriental Beef Skillet

- 1 pound beef round steak
- 2 tablespoons cooking oil *or* shortening
- 1 cup water
- 1/4 cup chopped onion
- 1 clove garlic, minced
- 1 teaspoon instant beef bouillon granules
- 1/8 teaspoon pepper
- 1 10-ounce package frozen cauliflower, thawed
- 1 cup thinly sliced carrot
- 1 6-ounce package frozen pea pods
- 3/4 cup cold water
- 2 tablespoons soy sauce
- 2 tablespoons cornstarch
- Hot cooked rice

Partially freeze meat (or partially thaw frozen meat). Allow 45 to 60 minutes to partially freeze a 1-inch-thick piece of meat. Thinly slice meat across the grain. In skillet brown meat slices quickly in hot cooking oil or shortening; remove from heat. Add the 1 cup water, onion, garlic, beef bouillon granules, and pepper. Cook and stir till bouillon is dissolved. Cut up any large pieces of cauliflower. Add cauliflower and sliced carrot to skillet; cover and simmer for 6 minutes. Stir in pea pods. Cover and continue cooking for 3 minutes more or till cauliflower is just tender.

With slotted spoon, transfer meat and vegetables to heated serving dish; keep warm. Blend the 3/4 cup water, soy sauce, and cornstarch. Stir into pan juices. Cook and stir till thickened and bubbly. Pour over meat and vegetables; season to taste with salt and pepper. Pass additional soy sauce, if desired. Serve with hot cooked rice. Makes 4 servings.

Oven Steak and Vegetables

This saucy Swiss-steak-style entrée is fancy enough to serve guests—

- 1 to 1 1/2 pounds beef round steak, cut 3/4 inch thick
- 1/4 cup all-purpose flour
- 1 teaspoon salt
- 1/8 teaspoon pepper
- 2 tablespoons cooking oil *or* shortening
- 1 16-ounce can tomatoes, cut up
- 1/2 cup chopped onion
- 1/2 teaspoon dried dillweed
- 4 medium carrots, cut into strips
- 2 medium zucchini, sliced (2 cups)
- Hot cooked rice

Trim excess fat from meat. Cut meat into 6 serving-size pieces. In plastic bag combine *half* of the flour, the salt, and pepper. Shake meat pieces in flour mixture to coat.

In skillet brown meat in hot oil or shortening. Transfer meat to 12x7 1/2x2-inch baking dish; reserve drippings in skillet.

In same skillet blend remaining flour into pan drippings. Stir in *undrained* tomatoes, chopped onion, and dillweed. Cook and stir till thickened and bubbly. Pour mixture over meat. Add carrots. Cover and bake in 350° oven for 1 hour. Add sliced zucchini. Cover and continue baking 15 to 20 minutes more or till meat and vegetables are tender. Season to taste with salt and pepper. Serve with hot cooked rice. Pass pan juices. Makes 4 to 6 servings.

Baked with a hint of dill, *Oven Steak and Vegetables* is a winning family pleaser. It's great served with rice.

Minute Steak Toss

Stir the meat carefully to keep it from falling apart—

- ½ cup cold water
- ¼ cup soy sauce
- 3 tablespoons cornstarch
- 1½ teaspoons lemon juice
- 1½ teaspoons worcestershire sauce
- ¼ teaspoon pepper
- 1 pound beef cubed steaks, cut into ½-inch strips
- 2 carrots, cut into very thin julienne strips (about 1 cup)
- 2 tablespoons cooking oil *or* shortening
- 1 green pepper, cut into strips
- 10 cherry tomatoes, halved *or* 2 tomatoes, cut into wedges
- Hot cooked rice

In mixing bowl combine water, soy sauce, cornstarch, lemon juice, worcestershire sauce, and pepper; blend till smooth. Add meat strips, stirring to coat. Cover; let stand at room temperature for 1 hour, stirring once or twice. Drain meat well; reserve marinade.

In skillet quickly cook meat and carrots in hot oil or shortening for 5 to 6 minutes; stir frequently. Push meat and carrots to one side; add green pepper strips. Cook and stir 2 to 3 minutes more.

Add enough water to reserved marinade to make 1½ cups liquid. Add to vegetable-meat mixture in skillet. Cook and stir till thickened and bubbly. Gently stir in tomatoes; cook about 1 minute more or till heated through. Serve over hot cooked rice. Pass additional soy sauce, if desired. Makes 4 servings.

Herbed Beef Stroganoff

- 1½ pounds beef stew meat, cut into 1-inch cubes
- 2 tablespoons cooking oil *or* shortening
- 1¾ cups water
- 2 cloves garlic, minced
- 1 bay leaf
- 2 teaspoons instant beef bouillon granules
- 1 teaspoon dried thyme, crushed
- ¾ teaspoon salt
- ½ teaspoon dried oregano, crushed
- ¼ teaspoon pepper
- 4 medium carrots, cut into ½-inch pieces
- 4 stalks celery, cut into ½-inch pieces
- 2 medium onions, cut into thin wedges
- 1 cup dairy sour cream
- ⅓ cup all-purpose flour
- ¼ cup water
- Hot cooked noodles

Trim excess fat from meat. In Dutch oven brown meat in hot oil or shortening; remove from heat. Add the 1¾ cups water, garlic, bay leaf, beef bouillon granules, thyme, salt, oregano, and pepper. Bring to boiling; reduce heat. Cover and simmer for 1 hour.

Add carrots, celery, and onions. Cover and simmer about 30 minutes more or till meat and vegetables are tender. Remove bay leaf and discard.

Combine sour cream, flour, and the ¼ cup water. Blend about *2 cups* of the hot mixture into sour cream mixture; return to remaining hot mixture in pan. Cook and stir till thickened; *do not boil*. Serve over hot cooked noodles. Makes 6 to 8 servings.

Sweet and Spicy Ribs

- 3 pounds beef *or* pork spareribs
- 2 tablespoons cooking oil *or* shortening
- 1½ cups water
- 1 large onion, chopped (1 cup)
- 1 medium apple, cored and sliced into rings
- 2 cloves garlic, minced
- 2 tablespoons sugar
- 1½ teaspoons instant beef bouillon granules
- 1 teaspoon salt
- ¼ teaspoon pepper
- ⅛ teaspoon ground cloves
- 2 tablespoons cold water
- 2 tablespoons cornstarch
- ¼ teaspoon Kitchen Bouquet (optional)

Cut meat into 2- or 3-rib portions. In large heavy oven-going skillet or 4-quart Dutch oven brown ribs in hot oil or shortening, a few pieces at a time, for 3 to 4 minutes or till browned on both sides. Drain off excess fat. Return all ribs to pan. Add the 1½ cups water, the chopped onion, apple rings, garlic, sugar, beef bouillon granules, salt, pepper, and cloves. Cover and bake in 350° oven for 2 hours for beef ribs (or, 1½ hours for pork ribs) or till meat is tender. Remove ribs to heated serving platter; keep warm.

To make gravy, pour pan juices into measuring cup. Skim off fat. Add water, if necessary, to make 2 cups liquid. Return to pan. Blend the 2 tablespoons cold water and the cornstarch; stir into pan juices. Cook and stir till thickened and bubbly. Add Kitchen Bouquet, if desired. Serve gravy with ribs. Makes 4 to 6 servings.

Easy Family-Style Pizza

This pizza is heartier than most—

- 3 to 3½ cups frozen Herbed Meat Sauce (recipe at right)
- ¼ cup water
- 1 package active dry yeast
- ½ cup warm water (110° to 115°)
- 2½ cups Homemade Biscuit Mix (see recipe, page 73) *or* packaged biscuit mix
- Cornmeal (optional)
- 1½ cups shredded mozzarella cheese (6 ounces)
- Grated parmesan cheese (optional)

In saucepan combine frozen Herbed Meat Sauce and ¼ cup water; cover tightly. Cook over medium heat about 25 minutes or till thawed, breaking up with fork after 15 minutes. Bring to boiling. Uncover; cook meat sauce for 10 to 15 minutes more or till desired sauce consistency.

Meanwhile, soften yeast in ½ cup warm water; add Homemade Biscuit Mix or packaged biscuit mix. Mix well. Turn out onto lightly floured surface; knead 25 strokes. Cover; let rest for 10 minutes.

Grease a 15x10x1-inch baking pan; lightly sprinkle with cornmeal, if desired. Pat or roll dough out onto bottom and halfway up sides of prepared pan. Bake crust in 425° oven for 8 to 10 minutes.

Spread meat sauce mixture over baked pizza crust. Sprinkle with shredded mozzarella cheese. Bake in 425° oven about 10 minutes more or till mozzarella cheese is melted and pizza is heated through. Pass grated parmesan cheese, if desired. Makes 6 to 8 servings.

Herbed Meat Sauce

- 3 pounds ground beef *or* ground pork
- 4 medium onions, chopped
- 2 cloves garlic, minced
- 2 28-ounce cans tomatoes, cut up
- 2 15-ounce cans tomato sauce
- 1 tablespoon dried basil, crushed
- 1 tablespoon dried oregano, crushed
- 2 teaspoons salt
- 1 teaspoon sugar
- ¼ teaspoon pepper
- 2 4-ounce cans mushroom stems and pieces (optional)

In 4-quart Dutch oven cook meat, onion, and garlic till meat is browned; drain off fat. Add *undrained* tomatoes, tomato sauce, basil, oregano, salt, sugar, and pepper. Bring to boiling; reduce heat and simmer, uncovered, for 30 minutes. Stir in *undrained* mushrooms, if desired. Simmer about 15 minutes more or till desired consistency.

Divide sauce into three 3- to 3½-cup portions. Cool. Seal each portion in moisture-vaporproof freezer container. Label; freeze. Makes 9½ to 10½ cups.

Use frozen sauce* within 6 months for Italian-Style Spaghetti Sauce (below), Easy Family-Style Pizza, *or* Cheesy Lasagne with Spinach.

Italian-Style Spaghetti Sauce: In saucepan combine 3 to 3½ cups *frozen Herbed Meat Sauce* and ¼ cup *water*, cover tightly. Cook over medium heat about 25 minutes or till thawed; break up with fork after 15 minutes. Bring to boiling. Uncover; cook 5 to 10 minutes more or till desired consistency. Serve over *hot cooked spaghetti*. Pass *parmesan cheese*, if desired. Serves 6.

*To use the meat sauce without freezing, *omit* the ¼ cup water called for in each recipe.

Cheesy Lasagne with Spinach

Here's a hearty lasagne that will delight both family and friends—

- 3 to 3½ cups frozen Herbed Meat Sauce (recipe at left)
- ¼ cup water
- 1 10-ounce package frozen chopped spinach
- 2 beaten eggs
- 1½ cups cream-style cottage cheese
- ½ teaspoon salt
- 1 cup shredded mozzarella cheese (4 ounces)
- 8 to 10 lasagne noodles, cooked and drained (8 ounces)
- Snipped parsley

In saucepan combine frozen Herbed Meat Sauce and water; cover tightly. Cook over medium heat about 25 minutes or till thawed, breaking up with fork after 15 minutes. Bring to boiling. Uncover; cook for 10 to 15 minutes more or till desired sauce consistency.

Cook spinach according to package directions. Drain well, pressing out excess moisture. In mixing bowl stir together beaten eggs, cottage cheese, salt, and cooked spinach.

In 13x9x2-inch baking pan arrange *half* of the cooked lasagne noodles. Spread *half* of the meat sauce over noodles. Spoon the spinach mixture over meat sauce layer. Sprinkle with *half* of the mozzarella cheese. Repeat layers with remaining noodles and meat sauce. Reserve remaining mozzarella cheese.

Place pan of lasagne on baking sheet to catch any bubbling juices during baking. Cover; bake in 375° oven about 40 minutes or till bubbly. Top with remaining mozzarella; bake 5 minutes more. Let stand about 10 minutes before serving. Garnish with parsley, if desired. Makes 8 servings.

Hamburger-Rice Skillet

1 pound ground beef *or* ground pork
1 medium onion, sliced and separated into rings
1 medium green pepper, coarsely chopped
1 clove garlic, minced
1 cup medium grain rice
1 16-ounce can tomatoes, cut up
1 8-ounce can tomato sauce
1 teaspoon worcestershire sauce
½ teaspoon dried basil, crushed
½ cup shredded American cheese *or* process cheese spread (optional)

In skillet cook beef or pork, onion, green pepper, and garlic till meat is browned; drain off fat. Add rice; cook, stirring constantly, for 2 minutes. Add *undrained* tomatoes, tomato sauce, worcestershire, basil, 1½ cups *water*, and 1 teaspoon *salt*. Bring to boiling; reduce heat. Cover; simmer 25 to 30 minutes or till rice is tender; stir occasionally. Remove cover; sprinkle with shredded cheese, if desired. Makes 6 servings.

Saucy Stroganoff

1½ pounds ground beef *or* ground pork
½ cup chopped onion
1 4-ounce can mushroom stems and pieces, drained
1½ teaspoons instant beef bouillon granules
½ teaspoon worcestershire sauce
1 cup dairy sour cream
3 tablespoons all-purpose flour
¼ cup catsup
Hot cooked noodles

In skillet cook ground beef or pork and onion till meat is browned. Drain off fat. Stir in mushrooms, bouillon granules, worcestershire sauce, 1½ cups *water*, ½ teaspoon *salt*, and ⅛ teaspoon *pepper*. Bring to boiling; reduce heat. Cover and simmer for 15 minutes.

Combine sour cream and flour. Gradually blend some of the hot beef mixture into sour cream; return to skillet. Cook and stir till thickened; *do not boil*. Stir in catsup; heat through. Serve over hot cooked noodles. Sprinkle with snipped parsley, if desired. Makes 6 to 8 servings.

Tomato Soup Spaghetti Sauce

1 pound ground beef *or* ground pork
1 large onion, chopped
1 large green pepper, chopped
1 clove garlic, minced
2 10¾-ounce cans condensed tomato soup
1 16-ounce can tomatoes, cut up
1 bay leaf
½ teaspoon dried basil, crushed
½ teaspoon dried oregano, crushed
Hot cooked spaghetti
Grated parmesan cheese (optional)

In saucepan cook beef or pork, onion, green pepper, and garlic till meat is browned. Drain off fat.

Stir in tomato soup, *undrained* tomatoes, bay leaf, basil, oregano, ½ teaspoon *salt*, and ⅛ teaspoon *pepper*. Bring to boiling; reduce heat. Simmer, uncovered, about 30 minutes or till thickened to desired consistency, stirring occasionally. Discard bay leaf. Serve over hot cooked spaghetti. Pass parmesan cheese, if desired. Makes 4 or 5 servings.

Individual Hamburger Casseroles

Try using chopped broccoli, spinach, sliced cauliflower, mixed vegetables, or cut asparagus for the cooked vegetable—

1 pound ground beef *or* ground pork
½ cup chopped onion
1½ cups soft bread crumbs (2 slices)
¾ teaspoon salt
½ teaspoon dried thyme, crushed
⅛ teaspoon pepper
3 tablespoons margarine *or* butter
¼ cup all-purpose flour
½ teaspoon salt
2 cups *reconstituted* nonfat dry milk *or* milk
½ cup shredded American cheese *or* process cheese spread (2 ounces)
2 cups cooked vegetable (see suggestions above)
2 tablespoons margarine *or* butter, melted

In skillet cook ground beef or pork and onion till meat is browned; drain off fat. Stir in ½ *cup* of the soft bread crumbs, the ¾ teaspoon salt, the thyme, and pepper.

In saucepan melt the 3 tablespoons margarine or butter; blend in flour and the ½ teaspoon salt. Add milk all at once. Cook and stir till thickened and bubbly. Add cheese, stirring till melted. Stir in meat mixture and cooked vegetable.

Turn meat-vegetable mixture into six 1-cup individual casseroles. (If desired, refrigerate casseroles up to 24 hours.) Combine remaining bread crumbs with the 2 tablespoons melted margarine or butter. Sprinkle atop casseroles just before baking. Bake in 350° oven about 20 minutes or till heated through. (Bake about 35 minutes if chilled.) Makes 6 servings.

Beef-Zucchini Pie

Here's a savory pie you'll enjoy serving to your company—

Single-Crust Pastry (see recipe, page 77)
1 pound ground beef *or* ground pork
½ cup chopped onion
1 clove garlic, minced
1 teaspoon dried basil, oregano, savory, *or* marjoram, crushed
¾ teaspoon salt
⅛ teaspoon pepper
1½ pounds zucchini, coarsely shredded (5 cups)
2 slightly beaten eggs
1 cup cream-style cottage cheese
½ cup shredded American cheese *or* process cheese spread (2 ounces)
1 teaspoon worcestershire sauce
½ teaspoon salt
½ teaspoon dry mustard

Prepare pastry; fit into a 9-inch pie plate. Roll edges under; flute to make a high rim. (Do not prick.) Bake the pie shell in 450° oven for 8 to 10 minutes.

In skillet cook ground beef or pork, onion, and garlic till meat is browned; drain off fat. Add herb, the ¾ teaspoon salt, and the pepper. In covered saucepan cook zucchini in a small amount of boiling salted water for 3 to 5 minutes or till tender. Drain thoroughly, pressing out excess water (should have about 2 cups cooked and drained zucchini).

Combine eggs, cottage cheese, American cheese or process cheese spread, worcestershire, the ½ teaspoon salt, and the mustard; add zucchini. Turn meat mixture into pie shell; spoon zucchini mixture atop. Bake in 350° oven about 35 minutes or till zucchini mixture is set. Cool 10 minutes before serving. Serves 6.

Curried Meatballs with Pasta

1 beaten egg
3 tablespoons *reconstituted* nonfat dry milk *or* milk
¾ cup soft bread crumbs (1 slice)
¼ cup finely chopped onion
2 tablespoons snipped parsley
½ teaspoon salt
⅛ teaspoon pepper
1 pound ground beef *or* ground pork
Margarine, butter, *or* cooking oil
1 medium green pepper, cut into strips
1½ to 2 teaspoons curry powder
¼ cup all-purpose flour
½ teaspoon salt
Dash pepper
2½ cups *reconstituted* nonfat dry milk *or* milk
Hot cooked rice

In bowl combine egg and the 3 tablespoons milk; stir in bread crumbs, onion, parsley, ½ teaspoon salt, and ⅛ teaspoon pepper. Add ground beef or pork; mix well. Shape into 24 meatballs.

In large skillet brown meatballs; cover and cook over low heat for 10 minutes. Remove meatballs from skillet and set aside; keep warm. Reserve 2 tablespoons drippings in skillet (add margarine, butter, or cooking oil, if necessary).

Cook green pepper and curry powder in drippings till green pepper is crisp-tender. Stir in flour, ½ teaspoon salt, and dash pepper. Add the 2½ cups milk all at once. Cook and stir till thickened and bubbly. Return meatballs to skillet; cover and cook about 2 minutes more or till meatballs are heated through. Serve meatballs and sauce over hot cooked rice. Makes 4 to 6 servings.

Smothered Beef Patties and Noodles

Serve this guest-pleasing entrée the next time you entertain—

1 beaten egg
2½ cups *reconstituted* nonfat dry milk *or* milk
½ cup finely chopped onion
⅓ cup fine dry bread crumbs
1 teaspoon salt
¼ teaspoon ground nutmeg
1½ pounds ground beef *or* 1 pound ground beef and ½ pound ground pork
¼ cup all-purpose flour
¾ teaspoon salt
¼ teaspoon pepper
Hot cooked noodles *or* other pasta *or* rice
Snipped parsley (optional)

In mixing bowl combine beaten egg and ½ *cup* of the milk. Stir in chopped onion, fine dry bread crumbs, the 1 teaspoon salt, and the nutmeg. Add ground beef or combination of ground beef and pork; mix well. Shape meat mixture into six to eight patties about ¾-inch thick.

In skillet cook patties over medium heat for 5 to 7 minutes on each side, turning once. Remove cooked patties from skillet and set aside.

For sauce, reserve ¼ *cup* of the drippings in skillet. Stir in flour, the ¾ teaspoon salt, and the pepper; cook and stir till bubbly, scraping up browned bits from pan. Gradually stir in the remaining 2 cups milk. Cook and stir till thickened and bubbly.

Return meat patties to sauce in skillet; heat through. Serve patties with sauce over hot cooked noodles or rice. Sprinkle with some snipped parsley, if desired. Makes 6 to 8 servings

Savory Scotch Meat Loaves

Each loaf is shaped around a hard-cooked egg; also pictured on cover—

1 beaten egg
3/4 cup soft bread crumbs
1/4 cup finely chopped onion
1/4 cup finely chopped green pepper
1/2 teaspoon salt
Dash pepper
1 pound ground beef *or* ground pork
4 hard-cooked eggs
1/2 cup catsup
2 tablespoons water
1 teaspoon vinegar
1/2 teaspoon chili powder
1/4 teaspoon dried oregano, crushed
Shredded cheddar, mozzarella, *or* American cheese (optional)

In mixing bowl combine beaten egg, bread crumbs, chopped onion, chopped green pepper, salt, and pepper. Add ground beef or ground pork; mix well.

Shape *one-fourth* of the meat mixture around *each* hard-cooked egg, completely enclosing the egg. Arrange meat loaves in 8x8x2-inch baking pan. Bake in 350° oven for 30 minutes. Drain off excess fat.

For sauce, combine catsup, water, vinegar, chili powder, and oregano; pour over meat loaves. Bake in 350° oven for 15 minutes more, spooning sauce over loaves occasionally. If desired, top *each* loaf with some of the shredded cheese. Return to oven and heat till cheese melts. Makes 4 servings.

◀ Pictured are *Savory Scotch Meat Loaves* and *Cheesy Broccoli-Liver Bake* (see recipe, page 25).

Cheesy Meat Loaf

1 beaten egg
1/4 cup catsup
1 cup shredded American *or* Swiss cheese *or* process cheese spread (4 ounces)
3/4 cup soft bread crumbs (1 slice)
1/2 cup finely chopped onion
1/4 cup finely chopped green pepper
3/4 teaspoon salt
1/2 teaspoon dried thyme, crushed
1/8 teaspoon pepper
1 pound ground beef *or* ground pork

Combine egg and catsup; stir in cheese, bread crumbs, onion, green pepper, salt, thyme, and pepper. Add ground beef or pork; mix well. In 11x7½x2-inch baking dish shape meat mixture into a 6-inch round loaf. Bake in 350° oven about 1 hour or till done. Makes 4 to 6 servings.

Meat Loaves Florentine

1 10-ounce package frozen chopped spinach, thawed
2 beaten eggs
1/4 cup *reconstituted* nonfat dry milk *or* milk
1½ cups soft bread crumbs (2 slices)
1 cup shredded mozzarella cheese (4 ounces)
1/4 cup catsup
3/4 teaspoon salt
1/2 teaspoon dried oregano, crushed
1/8 teaspoon pepper
1½ pounds ground beef *or* ground pork

Drain spinach well. In mixing bowl combine spinach, eggs, and milk. Stir in bread crumbs, cheese, catsup, salt, oregano, and pepper. Add beef or pork; mix well. Form meat mixture into two 7x4-inch loaves. Place in 13x9x2-inch baking pan. Bake in 350° oven for 50 to 60 minutes or till done. Makes 6 to 8 servings.

Cheese-Burger Casserole

Canned soups add richness to this creamy home-style casserole—

1 pound ground beef *or* ground pork
1/2 cup chopped onion
1 clove garlic, minced
1 11-ounce can condensed cheddar cheese soup
1 10 3/4-ounce can condensed cream of mushroom *or* celery soup
1/2 cup *reconstituted* nonfat dry milk *or* milk
1/2 teaspoon dried basil, crushed
1/8 teaspoon pepper
2 cups elbow *or* tiny shell macaroni, cooked and drained
1 cup shredded American *or* Swiss cheese *or* process cheese spread (4 ounces)
1/4 cup fine dry bread crumbs
1 tablespoon margarine *or* butter, melted

In skillet cook ground beef or pork, chopped onion, and garlic till meat is browned; drain off excess fat. In large mixing bowl stir together soups, milk, basil, and pepper. Stir in beef-onion mixture; mix well. Fold in cooked and drained macaroni and shredded cheese. Turn mixture into a 2-quart casserole.

Combine bread crumbs and melted margarine or butter; sprinkle over casserole. Bake in 375° oven about 45 minutes or till heated through. Makes 6 servings.

Sweet-Sour Meatballs

- 1 beaten egg
- 3/4 cup soft bread crumbs (1 slice)
- 1/4 cup chopped onion
- 2 tablespoons *reconstituted* nonfat dry milk *or* milk
- 3/4 teaspoon salt
- 1 pound ground beef *or* ground pork
- 2 tablespoons cooking oil *or* shortening
- 1 8 1/4-ounce can pineapple chunks
- 1/3 cup bottled barbecue sauce
- 1/4 cup frozen orange juice concentrate, thawed
- 1/4 teaspoon salt
- Dash pepper
- 2 tablespoons cold water
- 1 tablespoon cornstarch
- 1 medium green pepper, cut into strips
- Hot cooked rice

In large mixing bowl combine the egg, bread crumbs, onion, milk, and the 3/4 teaspoon salt. Add ground beef or pork; mix well. Shape into 24 meatballs (about 1 tablespoon each). In large skillet brown meatballs in hot oil or shortening. Drain off excess fat. Drain pineapple, reserving syrup. Add enough water to reserved syrup to make 3/4 cup liquid.

Combine syrup mixture, barbecue sauce, orange juice concentrate, the 1/4 teaspoon salt, and pepper. Pour over meatballs in skillet. Bring to boiling. Reduce heat; cover and simmer for 15 minutes. Combine cold water and cornstarch. Stir into skillet. Cook and stir till thickened and bubbly. Add pineapple and green pepper. Cover and simmer about 3 minutes or till green pepper strips are crisp-tender. Serve over hot cooked rice. Makes 6 servings.

Chili

- 1 pound ground beef *or* ground pork
- 1 large onion, chopped
- 1 medium green pepper, chopped
- 1 clove garlic, minced
- 1 16-ounce can tomatoes, cut up
- 1 16-ounce can red kidney beans
- 1 15-ounce can tomato sauce
- 1 tablespoon chili powder
- 1/2 teaspoon dried basil, crushed
- 1/2 teaspoon worcestershire sauce

In Dutch oven cook beef, onion, green pepper, and garlic till meat is browned; drain off fat. Stir in *undrained* tomatoes, *undrained* beans, tomato sauce, chili powder, basil, worcestershire sauce, and 1/2 teaspoon *salt*. Bring to boiling; reduce heat. Cover; simmer about 30 minutes. Makes 4 to 6 servings.

Cheesy Vegetable Chowder

- 1 pound ground beef
- 1/2 cup chopped onion
- 2 medium potatoes, peeled and cubed (2 cups)
- 1 10-ounce package frozen peas and carrots *or* one 16-ounce can peas and carrots, drained
- 2 teaspoons instant beef bouillon granules
- 2 1/2 cups *reconstituted* nonfat dry milk *or* milk
- 3 tablespoons all-purpose flour
- 1 1/2 cups shredded American *or* Swiss cheese *or* process cheese spread (6 ounces)
- Buttered French bread slices (optional)

In 3-quart saucepan brown beef and onion. Drain off fat. Add potatoes, peas and carrots, bouillon granules, 1 1/2 cups *water*, 1/4 teaspoon *salt*, and 1/8 teaspoon *pepper* to meat mixture. Cover and simmer for 10 to 15 minutes or till vegetables are tender.

Blend 1/2 *cup* of the milk with the flour. Add to saucepan along with remaining milk. Cook and stir till thickened and bubbly. Add cheese; heat and stir just till cheese melts. Serve with slices of buttered French bread, if desired. Makes 6 to 8 servings.

Beef-Vegetable Soup

- 1 1/2 to 2 pounds beef short ribs
- 4 cups water
- 1 16-ounce can tomatoes, cut up
- 1 medium onion, chopped
- 1 tablespoon instant beef bouillon granules
- 1 bay leaf
- 1/2 teaspoon salt
- 1/2 teaspoon dried basil, crushed
- 1/2 teaspoon dried oregano, crushed
- 1/8 teaspoon pepper
- 2 cups shredded cabbage
- 2 medium potatoes, peeled and cubed
- 2 medium carrots, sliced
- 1 stalk celery, sliced
- 2 tablespoons snipped parsley

Trim excess fat from ribs. In Dutch oven brown ribs on all sides; drain off fat. Add the next 9 ingredients. Cover and simmer for 1 hour.

Add cabbage, potatoes, carrots, celery, and parsley. Cover; simmer 30 minutes more or till meat and vegetables are tender. Remove meat from bones. Chop meat; discard bones. Remove bay leaf. Skim excess fat from soup. Return meat to soup; heat through. Serves 6.

Kidney in Herb Sauce

This colorful entrée will remind you of a beef stroganoff—

- ¾ to 1 pound beef kidney
- 2 cups water
- ½ cup chopped onion
- 1 small clove garlic, minced
- 1 tablespoon instant beef bouillon granules
- ½ teaspoon dried thyme, crushed
- ¼ teaspoon salt
- ½ cup coarsely chopped carrot
- ½ cup coarsely chopped celery
- ½ cup dairy sour cream
- 3 tablespoons all-purpose flour
- Hot cooked noodles
- Snipped parsley (optional)

Remove membranes and hard parts from kidney; cut meat crosswise into ½-inch strips. In saucepan combine kidney strips, water, chopped onion, garlic, instant beef bouillon granules, thyme, and salt. Cover and cook over low heat for 1½ hours, stirring occasionally.

Stir in chopped carrot and celery. Cover and continue cooking about 25 minutes more or till kidney and vegetables are tender. Remove vegetables and kidney; keep warm. Strain pan juices. Add water to juices, if necessary, to make 1½ cups liquid. Blend together sour cream and flour; stir some of hot liquid into sour cream mixture. Return all to saucepan. Cook and stir till thickened; *do not boil.* Return vegetables and kidney to saucepan; heat through. Season to taste with salt and pepper. Serve over hot cooked noodles. Garnish with snipped parsley, if desired. Makes 4 servings.

Cheesy Broccoli-Liver Bake

Pictured on page 22—

- 1 pound sliced beef liver
- ¼ cup all-purpose flour
- 2 tablespoons margarine *or* butter
- 1 4-ounce can mushroom stems and pieces, drained, *or* 1 cup sliced fresh mushrooms
- ½ cup chopped onion
- 2 tablespoons margarine *or* butter
- 2 tablespoons all-purpose flour
- ¼ teaspoon salt
- Dash pepper
- 1½ cups *reconstituted* nonfat dry milk *or* milk
- ½ cup shredded American *or* Swiss cheese (2 ounces)
- 1 10-ounce package frozen cut broccoli, cooked and drained
- ¼ cup fine dry bread crumbs
- ¼ cup grated parmesan cheese
- 2 tablespoons snipped parsley
- 2 tablespoons margarine *or* butter, melted

Cut liver into 4 serving-size pieces. Sprinkle liver with a little salt and pepper; coat with the ¼ cup flour. In large skillet melt 2 tablespoons margarine. Add liver; cook quickly about 5 minutes or till browned, turning once. Remove liver; set aside. In same skillet cook mushrooms and onion about 3 minutes or till onion is tender but not brown, adding additional margarine, if necessary. Remove from heat; set aside.

In saucepan melt 2 tablespoons margarine; blend in the 2 tablespoons flour, salt, and pepper. Add milk all at once. Cook and stir till thickened and bubbly. Stir in American or Swiss cheese. Stir broccoli into *1 cup* of the cheese sauce; set aside remaining. Pour broccoli mixture into bottom of 10x6x2-inch baking dish; top with liver and cooked mushroom-onion mixture. Pour remaining cheese sauce over all. Combine bread crumbs, parmesan, parsley, and the 2 tablespoons melted margarine. Sprinkle over sauce. Bake in 350° oven for 25 to 30 minutes or till heated through. Makes 4 servings.

Creole Liver Skillet

- 2 to 4 slices bacon
- 1 small onion, sliced
- ¼ cup chopped green pepper
- 1 pound sliced beef liver, cut into bite-size pieces
- 1 16-ounce can tomatoes, cut up
- 1 teaspoon lemon juice
- 1 teaspoon worcestershire sauce
- 1 teaspoon prepared mustard
- ½ teaspoon salt
- ¼ teaspoon pepper
- 1 tablespoon cornstarch
- 1 tablespoon cold water
- Hot cooked rice

In 10-inch skillet cook bacon till crisp; drain, reserving 2 tablespoons drippings in skillet. Crumble bacon; set aside. Cook onion and green pepper in reserved drippings till onion is tender but not brown; push to one side of skillet. Add liver. Cook quickly for 2 to 3 minutes or till browned. Add *undrained* tomatoes, lemon juice, worcestershire sauce, mustard, salt, and pepper. Cover and simmer for 2 to 3 minutes. Blend cornstarch and water; add to liver mixture in skillet. Cook and stir till thickened and bubbly. Serve over hot cooked rice; sprinkle with bacon. Makes 4 or 5 servings.

Pork & Ham

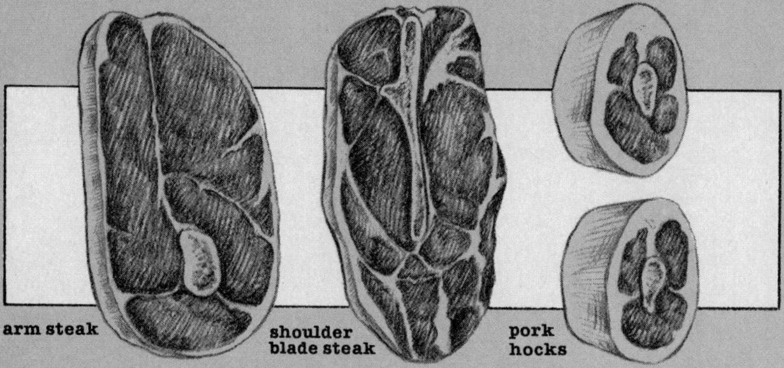

Meat is probably the most expensive item in your food budget and pork is no exception. The range in costs for different cuts of pork is great, and careful selection can result in real savings. The most economical pork cuts come from the shoulder—blade and arm steaks, the blade Boston roast, and fresh or smoked shoulder arm picnic. Pork cubed steaks, pork hocks, and ground pork are good buys, too. See the price chart on page 7 for the number of servings to plan on for these cuts.

Season It Well

Herbs and spices are economical ways to add zip to pork dishes. Add them in small amounts: For each 4 servings, use 1/4 teaspoon of a crushed dried herb or a ground spice, or 3/4 teaspoon of a fresh snipped herb. Taste before adding more. Try these herbs and spices to complement pork or ham: cloves, curry, dry mustard, ginger, rosemary, sage, and thyme.

Smoked Pork and Ham

If you buy a ham (be aware of specials for the best price), the shank portion of the ham is usually a better buy than the butt portion. Although the shank has more bone than the butt portion, it is often attractively priced. Remember, you can get more than one meal from a shank ham half. The illustration (right) shows how to divide a 7-pound shank ham half for 3 delicious meals if you use the cuts these ways:

—Use section 1 for soups and stews. Or, cube or grind the meat for casseroles, salads, and sandwiches.

—Section 2 is boneless. Uncut, this section is ideal for baking. Sliced, it can be fried or broiled. Cubed, it can be used in casseroles, soups, stews, or salads.

—Bake section 3. Add a touch of flavor with a glaze or sauce.

Smoked pork shoulder arm picnic is often confused with ham, as it is prepared similarly and its flavor is much like that of ham. It is often much less expensive per pound than ham, so compare prices. Follow package directions for cooking; some smoked meats are labeled "fully cooked"; others are labeled "cook before eating."

Buying bacon? It's a great way to add a flavor boost to many foods, but it's not considered a good enough protein source to qualify as a main dish on its own.

—Don't compare prices by cost per package. Package sizes differ, so look at the cost per pound.

—Regular-sliced bacon averages 20 to 22 slices per pound compared with about 12 slices per pound for thick-sliced bacon.

—Buy bacon "ends and pieces" if you plan to cut up the bacon for use; they're less expensive.

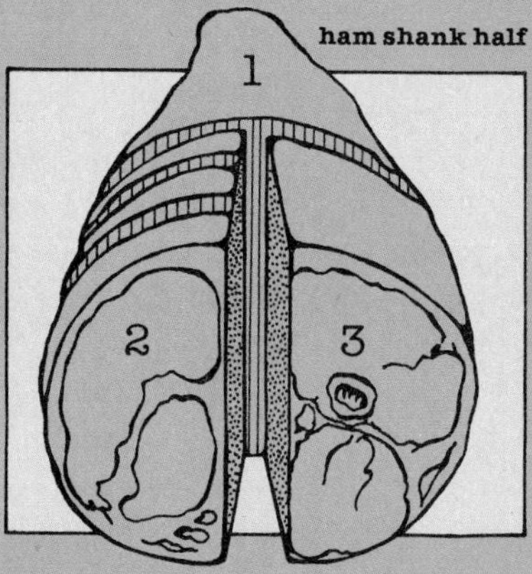

Nutrition

Pork is a good value nutritionally, too. Besides being rich in high-quality protein and iron, it is an excellent source of thiamin.

Pork Roast Dinner

- 1 3- to 4-pound pork shoulder blade Boston roast
- 2 tablespoons cooking oil *or* shortening
- 2 cups water
- 1 medium onion, cut into thin wedges
- 2 teaspoons instant beef bouillon granules
- 1½ teaspoons dried rosemary *or* thyme, crushed
- ½ teaspoon salt
- ½ teaspoon garlic powder
- ¼ teaspoon pepper
- 4 medium potatoes, peeled and halved
- 4 medium carrots, cut into 1½-inch pieces
- 1 9-ounce package frozen cut green beans
- ⅓ cup cold water
- ¼ cup all-purpose flour
- ¼ teaspoon Kitchen Bouquet (optional)

In Dutch oven brown meat on all sides in hot cooking oil or shortening. Drain off excess fat. Add the 2 cups water, onion wedges, beef bouillon granules, rosemary or thyme, salt, garlic powder, and pepper. Bring to boiling; reduce heat. Cover and simmer about 1½ hours or till meat is nearly tender. Add potatoes and carrots to meat. Simmer for 30 minutes. Add green beans and simmer about 15 minutes more or till meat and vegetables are tender. Remove meat and vegetables to heated platter; keep warm. To prepare gravy, skim fat from pan juices; reserve 2 cups juices. Blend the ⅓ cup cold water into flour; stir into reserved pan juices. Cook and stir till thickened and bubbly. Add Kitchen Bouquet, if desired; cook and stir 1 to 2 minutes more. Season to taste with salt and pepper. Pass gravy with meat. Makes 12 to 16 servings.

Barbecue-Sauced Shoulder Arm Picnic

Remove the skin from the shoulder arm picnic before basting with the sauce to let the barbecue flavor penetrate the meat—

- 1 3- to 4-pound fully cooked smoked pork shoulder arm picnic
- ½ cup catsup
- ⅓ cup chopped onion
- ¼ cup molasses
- 2 tablespoons water
- 2 tablespoons vinegar
- 1 teaspoon worcestershire sauce
- 1 teaspoon prepared mustard
- ½ teaspoon chili powder
- Snipped parsley (optional)

Remove skin from shoulder arm picnic, if present. Place shoulder arm picnic, fat side up, on a rack in shallow roasting pan.

Insert meat thermometer into center of thickest portion of meat, making sure bulb does not rest in fat or touch bone. Bake in 325° oven for 1 hour.

Meanwhile, prepare barbecue sauce. In small saucepan combine catsup, chopped onion, molasses, water, vinegar, worcestershire sauce, prepared mustard, and chili powder. Simmer, uncovered, about 15 minutes or till onion is tender, stirring occasionally.

Spoon some of the barbecue sauce over shoulder arm picnic. Continue baking about 30 minutes more or till meat thermometer registers 140°, basting 2 or 3 times with barbecue sauce. Garnish shoulder arm picnic with snipped parsley, if desired. Pass the remaining barbecue sauce with meat. Makes 12 to 16 servings.

Pineapple-Sauced Ham and Potatoes

There's enough meat to feed 8 to 10 tonight, with leftovers for tomorrow—

- 1 5- to 6-pound fully cooked ham shank portion
- 2 pounds sweet potatoes (6 medium)
- 1 20-ounce can crushed pineapple
- 2 tablespoons brown sugar
- 1 tablespoon cornstarch
- ⅛ teaspoon ground cloves
- Dash salt
- 2 tablespoons chili sauce *or* catsup
- 2 tablespoons margarine *or* butter

Place ham, fat side up, on a rack in shallow roasting pan. Insert meat thermometer into thickest portion of ham, making sure bulb does not rest in fat or touch bone. Bake in 325° oven for 1¼ hours.

Meanwhile, cook sweet potatoes in boiling salted water till tender; drain and cool. Peel sweet potatoes; halve lengthwise.

To make sauce, drain crushed pineapple, reserving syrup. Add water to reserved syrup if necessary to make 1 cup liquid. In saucepan blend together brown sugar, cornstarch, cloves, and salt. Add reserved pineapple liquid and chili sauce or catsup; cook and stir till thickened and bubbly. Stir in crushed pineapple and margarine or butter.

Drain fat from roasting pan; arrange cooked sweet potatoes around ham. Spoon some of the pineapple sauce over ham and potatoes. Bake for 30 to 45 minutes more or till meat thermometer registers 140°, basting occasionally with sauce. Heat any remaining sauce to pass with ham and sweet potatoes. Makes 8 to 10 servings.

Orange Pork Steaks

- 4 pork blade *or* arm steaks, cut ½ inch thick (2 pounds)
- 2 tablespoons cooking oil *or* shortening
- 4 medium sweet potatoes, peeled and cut lengthwise into ½-inch-thick slices
- 1 medium orange, peeled and thinly sliced
- ⅓ cup packed brown sugar
- ⅓ cup orange juice
- ⅛ teaspoon ground cinnamon
- ⅛ teaspoon ground nutmeg

Cut each pork steak into 2 serving-size pieces. In skillet slowly brown meat on both sides in hot oil or shortening. Sprinkle with salt and pepper. In 12x7½x2-inch baking dish arrange sweet potatoes. Place orange slices atop potatoes; cover with pork steaks.

For sauce, combine brown sugar, orange juice, cinnamon, nutmeg, and dash *salt*; pour over steaks. Cover; bake in 350° oven for 45 minutes. Uncover; continue baking about 30 minutes more or till meat and sweet potatoes are tender. Transfer to platter; spoon sauce over. Garnish with parsley, if desired. Makes 8 servings.

Marinated Pork Steaks

- 3 pork blade *or* arm steaks, cut ½ inch thick (1½ pounds)
- ½ cup soy sauce
- 2 tablespoons brown sugar
- 2 tablespoons lemon juice
- 2 tablespoons worcestershire sauce
- 2 tablespoons cooking oil
- 1 garlic clove, minced

Place pork steaks in shallow dish. For marinade, combine soy sauce, brown sugar, lemon juice, worcestershire sauce, cooking oil, garlic, and ⅓ cup *water*. Pour over pork steaks. Cover and refrigerate for several hours or overnight; turn steaks occasionally.

Drain pork steaks, reserving marinade. Place steaks on unheated rack of broiler pan. Broil steaks 3 inches from heat for 8 minutes; brush occasionally with marinade. Turn; broil 8 to 10 minutes more or till done, brushing occasionally with marinade. (Or, grill marinated steaks over *medium* coals for 10 minutes; brush occasionally with marinade. Turn; grill 8 to 10 minutes more or till steaks are done, brushing occasionally with marinade.) To serve, cut each pork steak into 2 serving-size pieces. Makes 6 servings.

Pork Chop and Pasta Dinner is a zesty oven-going entrée.

Pork Chop and Pasta Dinner

Try a different shaped pasta in this well-seasoned entrée, also pictured on the cover—

- 1½ cups corkscrew macaroni *or* elbow macaroni
- 6 pork rib chops, cut ½ inch thick
- 2 tablespoons cooking oil *or* shortening
- 1 15-ounce can tomato sauce
- ¼ cup chopped onion
- 1 teaspoon worcestershire sauce
- ½ teaspoon dried basil, crushed
- ¼ teaspoon sugar
- ¼ teaspoon salt
- ¼ teaspoon garlic powder
- ¼ teaspoon dried oregano, crushed
- Dash pepper
- ¼ cup grated parmesan cheese

Cook macaroni in boiling salted water according to package directions; drain. Place macaroni in 12x7½x2-inch baking dish.

In skillet brown chops in hot cooking oil or shortening; drain off excess fat. Season with a little salt and pepper. Arrange chops over macaroni in baking dish. Combine tomato sauce, onion, worcestershire sauce, basil, sugar, salt, garlic powder, oregano, and pepper; pour over chops and macaroni. Sprinkle with parmesan cheese. Cover and bake in 350° oven for 1 to 1¼ hours or till meat is tender. Serve with additional parmesan cheese, if desired. Serves 6.

Forgotten Pork Stew

Just mix up this stew, put it in the oven, and "forget it" till it's done—

- 1½ pounds pork stew meat, cut into 1-inch cubes
- 3 medium carrots, cut into ¾-inch pieces
- 3 medium potatoes, peeled and quartered
- 2 stalks celery, sliced
- 1 medium onion, chopped
- 1 10-ounce package frozen lima beans, thawed
- 1 10¾-ounce can condensed tomato soup
- ½ cup water
- 2 tablespoons quick-cooking tapioca
- 1 teaspoon salt
- ½ teaspoon dried basil, crushed
- ¼ teaspoon garlic powder
- ¼ teaspoon cayenne

In Dutch oven combine meat, carrots, potatoes, celery, onion, and lima beans. Combine tomato soup, water, tapioca, salt, basil, garlic powder, and cayenne. Add to Dutch oven; stir to combine. Cover and bake in 325° oven for 2 to 2¼ hours or till meat and vegetables are tender. Makes 8 servings.

Pork Burger Cups

- 1 beaten egg
- 3/4 cup soft bread crumbs (1 slice)
- 3/4 teaspoon salt
- 1/8 teaspoon garlic salt
- 1 pound ground pork *or* ground beef
- 1 4-ounce can mushroom stems and pieces
- 3 slices bacon
- 1 8-ounce can tomato sauce
- 1 cup shredded American cheese *or* process cheese spread (4 ounces)
- 1/2 cup finely chopped onion
- 1/2 teaspoon sugar
- 1/4 teaspoon dried thyme, crushed
- 1/4 teaspoon dried oregano, crushed

For burger cups, combine egg, bread crumbs, salt, and garlic salt. Add ground pork or beef; mix well. Divide into fourths. On 4 squares of waxed paper pat meat into four 5-inch rounds. Shape each over inverted 6-ounce custard cup; peel off paper. Chill 1 hour in refrigerator in shallow baking pan. Bake in 375° oven for 20 minutes.

Meanwhile, drain and coarsely chop mushrooms. In small skillet cook bacon till crisp; drain and crumble. Drain skillet; return bacon to skillet. Add mushrooms, tomato sauce, 1/2 *cup* of the cheese, the chopped onion, sugar, thyme, and oregano. Simmer for 5 minutes; stir occasionally.

Carefully remove meat from custard cups. Arrange on oven-going serving platter. Spoon about 1/3 *cup* of the sauce mixture into each burger cup. Sprinkle remaining shredded cheese atop. Broil filled burger cups 3 inches from heat about 4 minutes or till cheese is melted. Makes 4 servings.

Chili Burgers

- 1 7 1/2-ounce can tomatoes, cut up
- 1/2 cup crushed saltine crackers (10 crackers)
- 1 teaspoon salt
- 1 teaspoon chili powder
- 1/8 teaspoon pepper
- 1 pound ground pork *or* ground beef
- 3/4 cup shredded monterey jack *or* American cheese *or* process cheese spread (3 ounces)
- 1/4 cup finely chopped onion
- 2 tablespoons finely chopped green pepper
- 1 tablespoon margarine *or* butter
- 1 teaspoon cornstarch
- 1/4 teaspoon sugar
- 1/8 teaspoon salt
- Several dashes bottled hot pepper sauce
- 6 hamburger buns, split and toasted

Drain tomatoes, reserving liquid; set aside. Combine crushed crackers, 1/4 *cup* of the reserved tomato liquid, the 1 teaspoon salt, chili powder, and pepper. Add ground pork or beef; mix well. Form meat mixture into six patties that are 1/2-inch-thick.

Place on unheated rack of broiler pan; broil patties 3 inches from heat for 7 minutes. Turn; broil for 7 to 8 minutes more or till done, topping each patty with some of the shredded cheese the last minute of broiling.

Meanwhile, prepare sauce. In small saucepan cook chopped onion and green pepper in margarine or butter till tender but not brown. Blend in cornstarch. Stir in tomatoes, remaining reserved tomato juice, sugar, 1/8 teaspoon salt, and hot pepper sauce. Cook and stir over medium heat till bubbly. Serve patties in toasted buns; top with sauce. Makes 6 servings.

Pork and Cheese Turnovers

- 3 cups all-purpose flour
- 1 cup shortening
- 7 to 8 tablespoons cold water
- 3/4 pound ground pork *or* ground beef
- 1/2 cup chopped onion
- 1/2 of a 10-ounce package frozen mixed vegetables, cooked and drained
- 2/3 cup plain yogurt
- 2 teaspoons all-purpose flour
- 1/4 teaspoon dried thyme, crushed
- 1/4 teaspoon ground sage
- 1 1/2 cups shredded Swiss *or* mozzarella cheese
- Milk *or* water

Stir together 3 cups flour and 1 1/2 teaspoons *salt*. Cut in shortening till pieces are the size of small peas. Sprinkle *1 tablespoon* water over part of the mixture; toss with a fork. Repeat till all is moistened. Form dough into a ball.

For meat filling, in skillet cook ground pork or beef and onion till meat is browned. Drain. Add mixed vegetables. Combine yogurt, 2 teaspoons flour, thyme, sage, and 3/4 teaspoon *salt*. Stir into meat mixture. Add cheese; mix well.

Divide dough into 6 portions. On lightly floured surface roll one portion of dough to a 10x5-inch rectangle. Place on ungreased baking sheet. Beginning at short side, spoon about 2/3 *cup* filling on *half* of the rectangle. Moisten edges of pastry with a little milk or water. Fold dough over filling to make a square. Seal edges using tines of fork; cut slits in top. Repeat with remaining dough and filling. Brush tops with additional milk, if desired. Bake in 375° oven 35 to 40 minutes or till golden. Makes 6.

Oriental Pork and Rice

Strain and save the oil or shortening from frying, and use it again—

- 1/4 teaspoon instant chicken bouillon granules
- 1 beaten egg
- 1/4 cup cornstarch
- 1/4 cup all-purpose flour
- 1 tablespoon sesame seed (optional)
- 1 pound boneless pork, cut into 3/4-inch cubes
- Cooking oil *or* shortening for deep-fat frying
- 1 20-ounce can pineapple chunks
- 2 medium carrots, thinly bias sliced (1 cup)
- 1/2 cup catsup
- 2 tablespoons sugar
- 2 tablespoons cornstarch
- 2 tablespoons vinegar
- 1 tablespoon soy sauce
- 3/4 teaspoon instant chicken bouillon granules
- 1 large green pepper, cut into 3/4-inch squares
- Hot cooked rice

Dissolve 1/4 teaspoon bouillon granules in 1/4 cup *hot water*; cool slightly. Combine egg, 1/4 cup cornstarch, flour, and bouillon mixture; beat till smooth. Stir in sesame seed, if desired. Dip pork cubes in batter. Fry in deep hot fat (365°) for 5 to 6 minutes or till golden. Drain; keep warm.

Drain pineapple, reserving liquid; add water to make 1 1/2 cups liquid. In saucepan combine pineapple liquid and carrots. Bring to boiling; reduce heat. Cover; simmer for 5 to 7 minutes or till crisp-tender. Combine catsup and next 5 ingredients; stir into carrot mixture. Add green pepper and pineapple; cook and stir till thickened and bubbly. Stir in pork. Serve with rice; pass additional soy sauce, if desired. Makes 6 servings.

Cheesy Pork Steak Rolls

- 1 medium green pepper, chopped (3/4 cup)
- 2 tablespoons finely chopped onion
- 2 tablespoons margarine *or* butter
- 3 cups dry bread cubes
- 1 7 1/2-ounce can tomatoes, cut up
- 1 cup cubed *or* shredded Swiss cheese (4 ounces)
- 1/2 teaspoon salt
- 1/2 teaspoon poultry seasoning *or* ground sage
- 1/8 teaspoon pepper
- 6 pork cubed steaks

Cook green pepper and onion in margarine or butter till tender but not brown. Toss with bread cubes, *undrained* tomatoes, cheese, salt, poultry seasoning or sage, and pepper; mix well. Sprinkle meat with salt. Divide stuffing mixture among steaks. Roll up jelly roll-style; secure with wooden picks, if necessary. Place in 12x7 1/2x2-inch baking dish. Bake in 400° oven about 40 minutes or till done. Makes 6 servings.

Quiche a la Pork

- Single-Crust Pastry (see recipe, page 77)
- 3 beaten eggs
- 1 1/2 cups *reconstituted* nonfat dry milk *or* milk
- 1/4 teaspoon dried thyme, crushed
- 1 1/2 cups shredded American *or* Swiss cheese *or* process cheese spread (6 ounces)
- 1/2 cup coarsely chopped cooked pork
- 1/2 cup desired cooked vegetable, such as peas, chopped broccoli, spinach, *or* carrots

Prepare and roll out pastry; fit into a 9-inch pie plate. Trim and flute edges of pastry; do not prick. Line the unpricked shell with double thickness of heavy-duty foil. Bake in 450° oven for 5 minutes. Remove heavy-duty foil; bake 5 minutes more. Remove from oven; reduce heat to 325°.

Meanwhile, prepare filling. In bowl thoroughly combine eggs, milk, thyme, and 1/2 teaspoon *salt*. Stir in shredded cheese, chopped pork, and cooked vegetable. Pour into warm pastry shell. To prevent overbrowning, cover pastry edge with foil. Bake in 325° oven 45 to 50 minutes or till knife inserted near center comes out clean. Let stand 10 minutes before serving. Makes 4 to 6 servings.

Chow Mein Pork Salad

This crunchy salad is easy to prepare and makes good use of leftover pork—

- 2 cups cubed cooked pork
- 1 cup shredded carrot
- 1 cup chopped celery
- 1 cup chopped green pepper
- 1/3 cup chopped onion
- 2/3 cup salad dressing *or* mayonnaise
- 1 tablespoon lemon juice
- 1 teaspoon prepared mustard
- 1/4 teaspoon salt
- Dash pepper
- 1 3-ounce can (2 1/4 cups) chow mein noodles
- Lettuce cups

In mixing bowl combine cubed pork, shredded carrot, chopped celery, green pepper, and onion. Combine salad dressing or mayonnaise, lemon juice, prepared mustard, salt, and pepper; add to meat and vegetable mixture. Mix well. Cover and chill. Add chow mein noodles just before serving; toss. Serve spooned into lettuce cups. Makes 4 to 6 servings.

Cheesy Ham and Vegetable Chowder

- 5 cups water
- 2 10¾-ounce cans condensed cream of mushroom soup
- 1 cup coarsely chopped fully cooked ham *or* fully cooked smoked pork shoulder arm picnic
- 1 8¾-ounce can whole kernel corn
- ½ of a 10-ounce package frozen cut broccoli
- ⅓ cup finely chopped onion
- ⅓ cup shredded carrot
- 1½ cups nonfat dry milk *powder*
- ¼ cup all-purpose flour
- 1 cup shredded American cheese *or* process cheese spread (4 ounces)

In Dutch oven combine *3 cups* of the water, the mushroom soup, ham or smoked picnic, *undrained* corn, broccoli, onion, and carrot; mix well. Bring to boiling. Reduce heat; cover and simmer for 8 to 10 minutes or till broccoli is tender. Combine the remaining 2 cups water, dry milk powder, and flour; stir into soup mixture. Cook and stir till thickened and bubbly. Add cheese; cook and stir till cheese is melted. Makes 8 servings.

Ham and Pasta

- 4 medium carrots, thinly bias sliced
- 1½ cups cubed fully cooked ham *or* fully cooked smoked pork shoulder arm picnic
- 8 ounces spaghetti *or* fettuccine *or* other pasta
- ¼ teaspoon instant chicken bouillon granules
- ½ cup grated parmesan cheese
- ½ cup dairy sour cream
- ¼ cup margarine *or* butter, melted
- ¼ cup snipped parsley

Cook carrots in boiling salted water for 10 minutes or till crisp-tender; drain well. Add ham or smoked shoulder arm picnic; cover and keep warm. Meanwhile, cook pasta according to package directions till tender.

Dissolve chicken bouillon granules in ¼ cup *boiling water*; combine with parmesan cheese, sour cream, and margarine or butter. Stir in carrot-ham mixture and parsley. Drain pasta (do not rinse); transfer to warm serving platter. Toss with sour cream-ham mixture. Sprinkle with additional parmesan cheese, if desired. Makes 4 to 6 servings.

Ham-Vegetable Toss

- 2 cups coarsely chopped fully cooked ham
- 1 10-ounce package frozen whole kernel corn, cooked and drained *or* one 17-ounce can whole kernel corn, drained
- 1 10-ounce package frozen lima beans, cooked and drained *or* one 16-ounce can lima beans, drained
- 1 small onion, sliced and separated into rings
- ½ cup chopped celery
- ¼ cup chopped dill pickle
- ¼ cup salad oil
- 2 tablespoons vinegar
- 2 tablespoons catsup
- 1 teaspoon chili powder
- 1 teaspoon prepared mustard
- ¼ teaspoon sugar
- 4 cups torn lettuce

Combine ham, corn, lima beans, onion, celery, and pickle. In screw-top jar combine oil, vinegar, catsup, chili powder, mustard, sugar, and ½ teaspoon *salt*. Cover; shake to mix well. Toss with vegetable mixture; chill. Toss with lettuce just before serving. Makes 6 to 8 servings.

Deep-Dish Ham and Broccoli Pie

- 1 10-ounce package frozen cut broccoli
- ½ cup chopped onion
- 3 tablespoons margarine *or* butter
- 3 tablespoons all-purpose flour
- 1½ cups *reconstituted* nonfat dry milk *or* milk
- 1 cup shredded American cheese *or* process cheese spread (4 ounces)
- 2 teaspoons prepared mustard
- 1½ cups coarsely chopped fully cooked ham
- 1 cup all-purpose flour
- ¼ cup margarine *or* butter
- ¼ cup shortening
- 1 beaten egg
- Milk

Cook frozen broccoli according to package directions; drain well. Set aside. In saucepan cook onion in 3 tablespoons margarine or butter till tender but not brown. Blend in 3 tablespoons flour and dash *pepper*. Add milk all at once; cook and stir till thickened and bubbly. Add cheese and mustard, stirring to melt cheese. Stir in ham. In 2-quart casserole layer *half* of the broccoli, all of the ham mixture, and remaining broccoli.

In mixing bowl stir together the 1 cup flour and ½ teaspoon *salt*. Cut in ¼ cup margarine or butter and the shortening till pieces are the size of small peas. Add beaten egg; gently toss with fork till all of the mixture is moistened.

Form dough into a ball. On lightly floured surface roll dough to a 9-inch circle; place atop filling. Turn edges under and flute; cut slits for escape of steam. Brush with milk. Bake in 425° oven about 20 minutes or till pastry is golden. Let stand for 10 to 15 minutes before serving. Makes 6 servings.

Ham and Cheese Stuffed Potatoes

6 medium potatoes
1/3 cup chopped onion
1/3 cup chopped celery
1/4 cup margarine *or* butter
1/2 cup *reconstituted* nonfat dry milk *or* milk
1 teaspoon prepared mustard
1/4 teaspoon salt
1/8 teaspoon garlic powder
Dash pepper
3 cups diced fully cooked ham *or* fully cooked smoked pork shoulder arm picnic
3/4 cup shredded American cheese *or* process cheese spread (3 ounces)
1/4 cup fine dry bread crumbs
1 tablespoon margarine *or* butter, melted
1/2 teaspoon paprika

Scrub potatoes thoroughly and prick with a fork. Bake in 425° oven for 40 to 60 minutes or till potatoes are tender. Reduce oven temperature to 350°.

Meanwhile, in skillet cook chopped onion and celery in *half* of the margarine or butter till tender. Set aside.

Halve potatoes lengthwise. Scoop out insides, leaving 1/4-inch-thick potato shells; mash insides with the remaining margarine or butter. Beat in milk. Add prepared mustard, salt, garlic powder, and pepper; mix well. Stir in diced ham or smoked shoulder arm picnic, shredded cheese, and the onion and celery mixture. Spoon into potato shells; arrange in 13x9x2-inch baking pan. Mix fine dry bread crumbs, the 1 tablespoon melted margarine or butter, and the paprika; sprinkle atop shells. Bake in 350° oven about 30 minutes or till heated through. Makes 6 servings.

Spicy Ham Patties with Apple Rings

The nonfat dry milk powder adds an extra boost of protein to this main dish—

2 beaten eggs
1/2 cup applesauce
1 1/2 cups soft bread crumbs (2 slices)
1/3 cup nonfat dry milk *powder*
1/4 cup chopped onion
1/2 teaspoon dry mustard
1/4 teaspoon salt
3/4 pound ground fully cooked ham *or* ground fully cooked smoked pork shoulder arm picnic
1/2 pound ground pork
1 tablespoon brown sugar
2 teaspoons cornstarch
1/4 teaspoon dry mustard
Dash ground cloves
3/4 cup applesauce
1 tablespoon vinegar
1 medium apple, cored and sliced into 6 rings
Snipped parsley (optional)

In mixing bowl combine beaten eggs, the 1/2 cup applesauce, and the bread crumbs; stir in nonfat dry milk powder, chopped onion, 1/2 teaspoon dry mustard, and salt. Add ground ham or smoked shoulder arm picnic and ground pork; mix well. Shape meat mixture into 6 patties; place in 13x9x2-inch baking pan. Bake in 350° oven for 40 to 45 minutes or till done.

Meanwhile, prepare sauce. In saucepan combine brown sugar, cornstarch, 1/4 teaspoon dry mustard, and cloves. Blend in the 3/4 cup applesauce and the vinegar. Cook and stir till thickened and bubbly. Add apple rings; cover and simmer about 15 minutes or till apple rings are just tender. To serve, arrange an apple ring atop each patty. Spoon sauce over. Garnish with parsley, if desired. Makes 6 servings.

Spaghetti and Ham Bake

Your family will love this parmesan-flavored casserole—

8 ounces spaghetti *or* linguine *or* other pasta
1 small green pepper
1/4 cup chopped onion
3 tablespoons margarine *or* butter
3 tablespoons all-purpose flour
1 teaspoon instant chicken bouillon granules
1/8 teaspoon ground nutmeg
1 13-ounce can (1 2/3 cups) evaporated milk
3/4 cup water
1 1/2 cups coarsely chopped fully cooked ham *or* fully cooked smoked pork shoulder arm picnic
1/2 cup grated parmesan cheese

Cook spaghetti or other pasta in boiling salted water according to package directions. Drain and set aside. Chop *half* of the green pepper. Cut remaining pepper into strips for garnish; set aside.

For sauce, in medium saucepan cook the chopped green pepper and the onion in margarine or butter till tender but not brown. Blend in flour, chicken bouillon granules, and nutmeg. Add evaporated milk and the water all at once; cook and stir over medium heat till thickened and bubbly.

Combine drained pasta, sauce, chopped ham or smoked shoulder arm picnic, and 1/4 *cup* of the parmesan cheese. Turn pasta mixture into 10x6x2-inch baking dish. Sprinkle with remaining parmesan cheese. Bake in 350° oven for 25 to 30 minutes or till pasta mixture is heated through. Garnish with reserved green pepper strips. Makes 4 to 6 servings.

Sausage & Franks

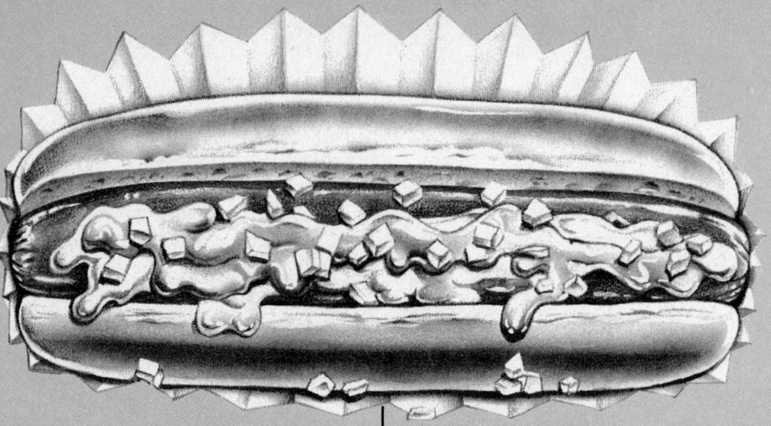

Sausages and franks are economical meats to include in budget meal planning. Both are good values; you can plan on 5 to 6 servings per pound as you don't pay for bone. Their nutritional profile is similar to other pork products and both are good sources of protein, iron, and the B vitamins. Some basic knowledge about the many varieties of sausage and franks available will help you create exciting main dishes within your budget.

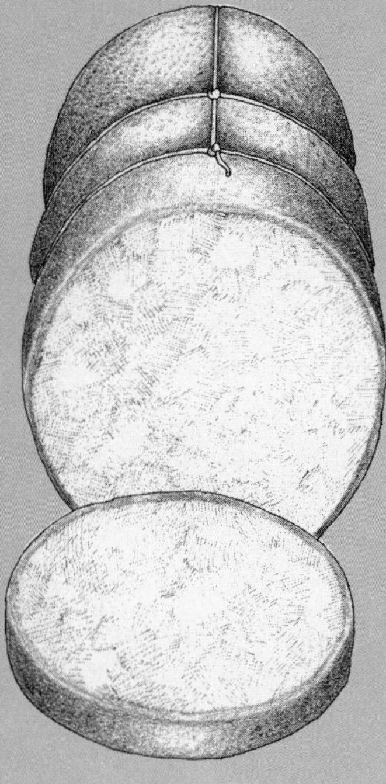

Sausage

Shop for sausage specials to find the best value. Most link sausages are interchangeable in recipes: You can use any of several sausage varieties as long as they are from the same group—fresh sausage, cooked or uncooked smoked sausage, or dry or semidry sausages. Their differences are:

Fresh sausage has not been cured, so keep it refrigerated; thoroughly cook it before eating. This type of sausage may be sold frozen. Bulk pork sausage, Italian sausage, and some bratwurst and fresh Polish sausages are examples.

Smoked sausage may be sold uncooked or, most commonly, fully cooked. Both need to be refrigerated until used. Prepare uncooked smoked sausage according to package directions; for fully cooked sausage simply heat through. Some smoked sausages to look for are bologna, knackwurst, smoked Polish sausage, and some salami.

Dry and semidry sausages are fermented and have a tangy flavor. Refrigerate semidry sausages; store dry sausages in a cool place. Sausages in this group include some salami, all summer sausage, and cervelat.

Don't forget bulk pork sausage. It generally costs less per pound than link sausage, so substitute it for link sausage where you can. For example, serve sausage patties instead of links for breakfast, or use cooked bulk pork sausage in casseroles instead of sliced link sausage.

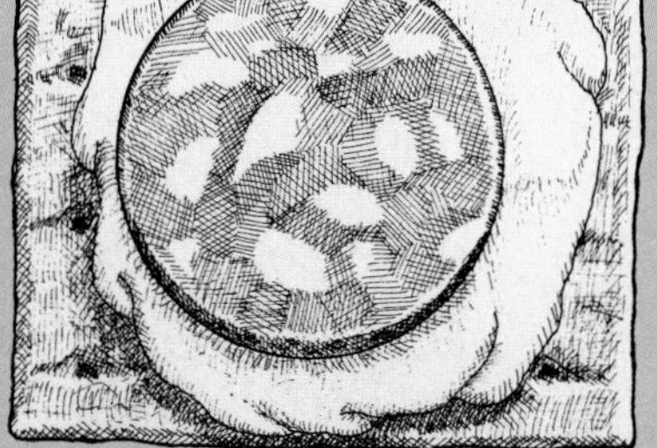

Franks

Frankfurters, hot dogs, and wieners are all different names for the same product. Franks are probably the best known—and the most used—sausage for cooking on a budget. With a wide variety of brands and sizes available, which are the best buy? Knowing that franks have minimum standards for their ingredients, your best value will be in the lowest cost franks per pound. (Since package sizes differ, compare cost per pound, not per package.) Check the list of ingredients to find out what you're getting; some are a combination of pork and beef, and others are all beef. Some franks are even made of ground turkey.

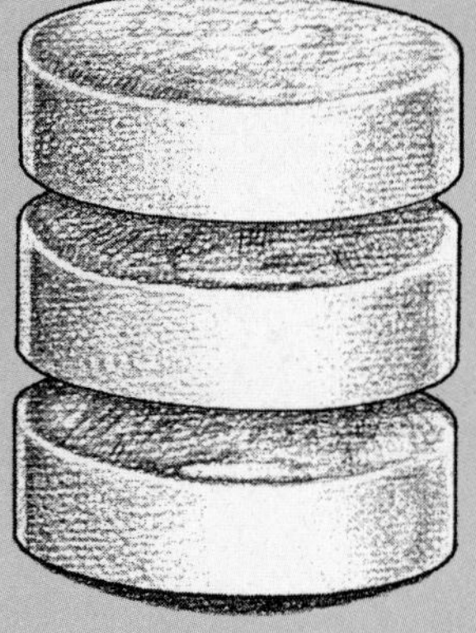

And franks are easy to prepare; they can be simmered, broiled, pan-broiled, or stuffed. Serve them whole as the main dish, add them to a casserole or skillet dish, or substitute them for other fully cooked sausage links in various recipes.

Cheesy Stuffed Peppers

Pictured on pages 10 and 11—

- 1 cup tiny shell macaroni *or* elbow macaroni
- 6 large green peppers
- 1 pound bulk pork sausage
- 1/3 cup chopped onion
- 3 tablespoons all-purpose flour
- 1/2 teaspoon dried basil, crushed
- 1 15-ounce can tomato sauce
- 1 8 3/4-ounce can whole kernel corn
- 1 cup shredded American cheese or process cheese spread (4 ounces)
- 3/4 cup soft bread crumbs (1 slice)
- 1 tablespoon margarine *or* butter, melted

Cook macaroni according to package directions; drain and set aside. Cut tops from green peppers; discard seeds and membranes. (Reserve tops for another use.) Cook peppers in boiling salted water for 3 to 5 minutes; invert to drain. Sprinkle insides of peppers lightly with salt. Arrange in 12x7 1/2x2-inch baking dish.

In skillet cook sausage and onion till meat is browned and onion is tender. Push to one side. Drain off fat, reserving 3 tablespoons. In same skillet blend flour and basil into reserved drippings. Add tomato sauce and *undrained* corn. Cook and stir till thickened and bubbly. Stir in cheese till melted. Add cooked macaroni; mix well. Spoon into peppers. Mix bread crumbs and melted margarine or butter; sprinkle atop peppers. Bake in 350° oven for 25 to 30 minutes or till heated through. Makes 6 servings.

Sausage Brunch Bake

- 3/4 pound bulk pork sausage
- 6 beaten eggs
- 1 1/2 cups *reconstituted* nonfat dry milk *or* milk
- 2 slices bread, cut into 1/2-inch cubes
- 1 cup shredded American cheese *or* process cheese spread (4 ounces)
- 3/4 teaspoon dry mustard
- 1/2 teaspoon salt
- Dash pepper

In skillet cook sausage till browned; drain well. Combine eggs, milk, bread cubes, cheese, mustard, salt, and pepper. Add sausage. Pour into greased 8x1 1/2-inch round baking dish. Cover; refrigerate several hours or overnight. Bake in 350° oven about 45 minutes or till nearly set in center. Let stand 10 minutes before serving. Makes 4 to 6 servings.

Sausage-Vegetable Skewers

- 4 links fully cooked bratwurst (1 pound)
- 2 small tomatoes, quartered
- 1 small green pepper, cut into 1 1/2-inch squares
- 1/3 cup bottled barbecue sauce
- 2 tablespoons apricot preserves
- 2 teaspoons prepared mustard

Make diagonal cuts 1/4 inch deep every 1/2 inch in each bratwurst link. Cut each bratwurst crosswise into thirds. On 4 skewers alternately thread bratwurst pieces, tomato, and green pepper.

In small bowl stir together barbecue sauce, apricot preserves, and mustard. Arrange skewers on a baking sheet; broil 3 inches from heat for 8 to 10 minutes or till bratwurst is heated through, turning often and brushing frequently with barbecue sauce. (Or, grill kabobs over *medium* coals for 8 to 10 minutes or till bratwurst is heated through. Turn often and brush frequently with barbecue sauce mixture.) Serve kabobs with toasted Italian bread slices, if desired. Makes 4 servings.

Sausage-Kraut Stew

- 1 small onion, sliced
- 2 tablespoons margarine *or* butter
- 1 16-ounce can sauerkraut, snipped
- 1 7 1/2-ounce can tomatoes, cut up
- 2 medium potatoes, peeled and cubed
- 1 medium carrot, chopped
- 1/2 cup water
- 1 tablespoon brown sugar
- 1/2 teaspoon salt
- 1/2 teaspoon caraway seed
- 1/2 teaspoon instant chicken bouillon granules
- Dash pepper
- 12 ounces fully cooked smoked sausage, cut up

In large saucepan cook onion in margarine or butter till tender but not brown. Drain sauerkraut, reserving 1/2 cup liquid. Add sauerkraut, reserved liquid, *undrained* tomatoes, potatoes, carrot, water, brown sugar, salt, caraway, bouillon granules, and pepper to saucepan. Cover; simmer for 45 to 50 minutes or till vegetables are tender, stirring occasionally. Add sausage; cover and simmer about 5 minutes more or till sausage is heated through. Makes 4 to 6 servings.

Frank-Kraut Stew: Prepare Sausage-Kraut Stew as above *except* substitute 12 ounces *frankfurters*, cut up, for the sausage.

Autumn Sausage Meatball Skillet

2 medium sweet potatoes
1 beaten egg
1½ cups soft bread crumbs
1 pound bulk pork sausage *or* ground pork
1 tablespoon cooking oil
⅓ cup chopped celery
3 medium apples, peeled and cut into thin wedges
1 cup orange juice
¼ cup water
3 tablespoons brown sugar
1 tablespoon soy sauce
½ teaspoon salt
⅛ teaspoon ground cinnamon
¼ cup cold water
5 teaspoons cornstarch
Hot cooked rice *or* noodles (optional)

In covered saucepan cook sweet potatoes in boiling salted water for 30 to 40 minutes or till tender; drain. Cool slightly; peel and cut into 1-inch-thick pieces.

Meanwhile, prepare meatballs. In mixing bowl combine egg and bread crumbs. Add sausage or ground pork; mix well. Shape mixture into 1-inch meatballs. In skillet brown meatballs, a few at a time, in hot oil; set aside.

Drain off fat, reserving 1 tablespoon drippings in skillet. Cook celery in reserved drippings till crisp-tender; drain off fat. Return meatballs to skillet; add sweet potatoes, apples, orange juice, ¼ cup water, brown sugar, soy sauce, salt, and cinnamon. Bring to boiling; reduce heat. Cover; simmer 10 minutes. Blend the ¼ cup cold water into the cornstarch. Stir into meatball mixture. Cook and stir till thickened and bubbly. Serve with rice or noodles, if desired. Makes 4 to 6 servings.

◀ *Frank and Potato Bake* gets its smoothness from cheese and its tang from mustard.

Sausage Sandwich Italiano

1 pound bulk Italian sausage
½ cup chopped onion
½ cup chopped green pepper
1 clove garlic, minced
1 6-ounce can tomato paste
⅔ cup water
½ teaspoon dried basil, crushed
¼ teaspoon sugar
¼ teaspoon salt
4 slices mozzarella cheese, quartered
8 hamburger buns, split and toasted

In skillet cook Italian sausage, chopped onion, green pepper, and garlic till meat is browned and vegetables are tender. Drain off excess fat. Stir in tomato paste, water, basil, sugar, and salt. Simmer for 8 to 10 minutes, stirring occasionally.

Place a cheese quarter on bottom half of *each* bun. Spoon about ⅓ cup meat mixture on each bun. Top with second cheese quarter. Add tops of buns. Place sandwiches in 15x10x1-inch baking pan. Cover; bake in 350° oven for 15 to 20 minutes or till cheese is melted. Makes 8 sandwiches.

Tangy German Potato-Frank Salad

1 10¾-ounce can condensed cream of celery soup
⅓ cup nonfat dry milk *powder*
2 tablespoons sweet pickle relish
2 tablespoons vinegar
1 tablespoon finely chopped onion
½ teaspoon salt
Dash pepper
3 cups cubed cooked potatoes
8 ounces frankfurters, bias sliced into 1-inch pieces

In skillet combine celery soup, dry milk powder, sweet pickle relish, vinegar, onion, salt, pepper, and ⅓ cup *water*; bring to boiling. Reduce heat. Stir in cubed potatoes and sliced frankfurters; simmer about 10 minutes or till heated through. Garnish with snipped parsley, if desired. Makes 4 servings.

Frank and Potato Bake

¼ cup finely chopped onion
1 tablespoon margarine *or* butter
1 tablespoon all-purpose flour
½ teaspoon salt
⅔ cup *reconstituted* nonfat dry milk *or* milk
¾ cup shredded American cheese *or* process cheese spread (3 ounces)
1 tablespoon snipped parsley
2 teaspoons prepared mustard
8 ounces frankfurters, sliced (4 or 5)
4 medium potatoes, cooked, peeled, and sliced
Snipped parsley (optional)

In small saucepan cook onion in margarine or butter till tender but not brown. Blend in flour and salt. Add milk all at once; cook and stir over medium heat till thickened and bubbly. Add shredded cheese, stirring to melt.

Stir in 1 tablespoon snipped parsley and the mustard. Fold in sliced frankfurters and potatoes; turn into a 1-quart casserole. Cover and bake in 350° oven about 35 minutes or till heated through. Garnish with additional snipped parsley, if desired. Makes 4 servings.

Poultry

Poultry is one of the best meat buys for both your budget and nutrition. It's a real plus when trying to cut main-dish costs.

Cutting Up A Chicken

Nutritionally, not only is it rich in high-quality protein and iron, it is one of the best sources of niacin, a B vitamin. Poultry is also lower in fat than many other meats.

You can save several cents a pound by buying whole chickens and cutting them up. Here's how:

—Cut the skin between the body and thighs. Bend the legs until the bones break at the hip joints.

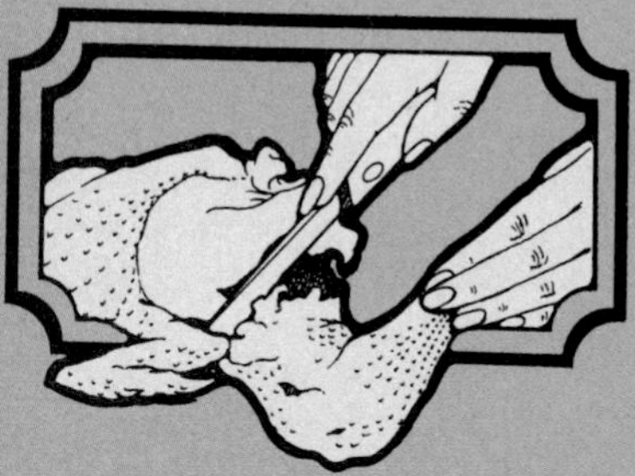

—Remove the leg and thigh pieces from the body by cutting with a sharp knife between the hip joints as close as possible to the backbone, as shown above.

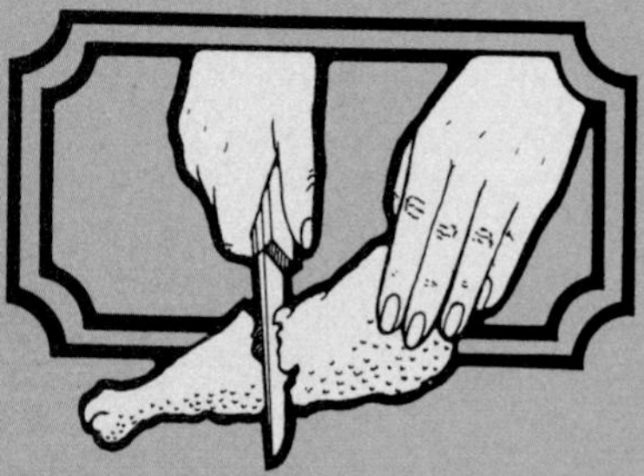

—Separate the thighs and legs by first cutting through the skin at the knee joint. Break the joint, then cut the thigh and leg apart, as shown.

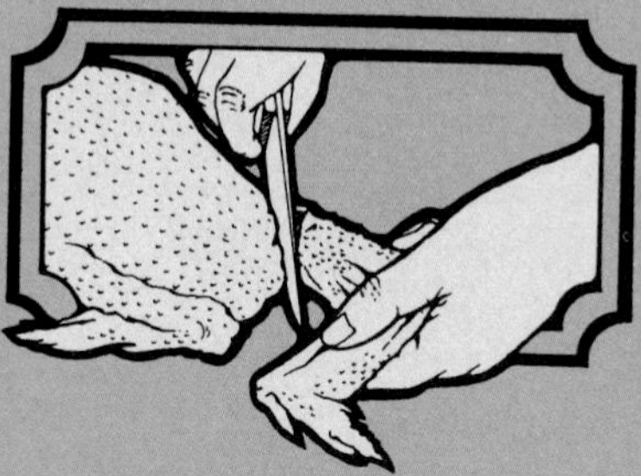

—To remove the wings from the body, cut through the skin on the inside of the wings at the joint. Break the joint, then cut the wings from the body, as shown.

—Divide the body, as shown above. Cut along the breast end of the ribs to the neck to separate the breast and back sections. Bend the back piece in half to break it at the joint; cut through the broken joint. Cut off the tail, if desired.

—Divide the breast into 2 lengthwise pieces by cutting along the breastbone.

Other Poultry Tips

—Family-size packages of cut-up chicken can be a bargain; watch for special prices on them.

—To feed a crowd, consider preparing a turkey; it has more meat and less bone and fat per pound than smaller birds.

—For maximum savings, buy the largest bird you can cook and store. Refrigerate leftovers up to 2 days for casseroles, soups, salads, and sandwiches. Freeze leftovers for up to 2 months.

—Begin a rich and tasty soup with a meat turkey frame to use every bit of meat on the bird.

Boning Chicken Breasts

Chicken breasts are a choice cut that always commands a higher price when packaged and bought as individual pieces. And, boneless chicken breasts cost even more.

Reserve the chicken breasts from whole broiler-fryers. By learning to skillfully bone chicken breasts yourself, you can save money on elegant main dishes that rate as company fare.

—First, remove the skin. Place one chicken breast half on cutting board, skin side up. Pull the skin away from the meat; discard skin. Repeat with remaining chicken breast halves.

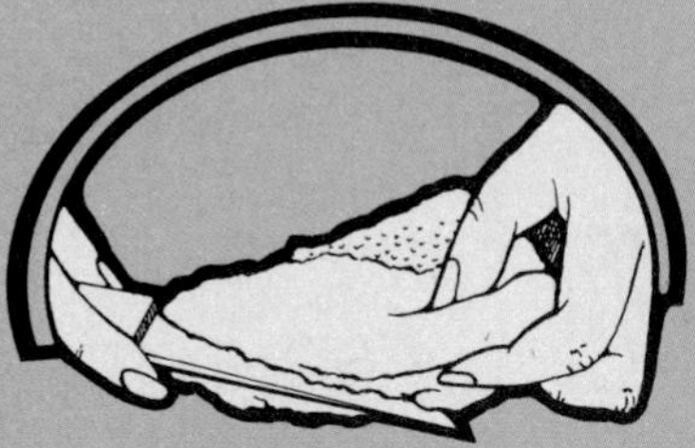

—Hold chicken breast half bone side down. Starting from the breastbone side of breast, cut meat away from bone. Cut as close to the bone as possible, as shown above.

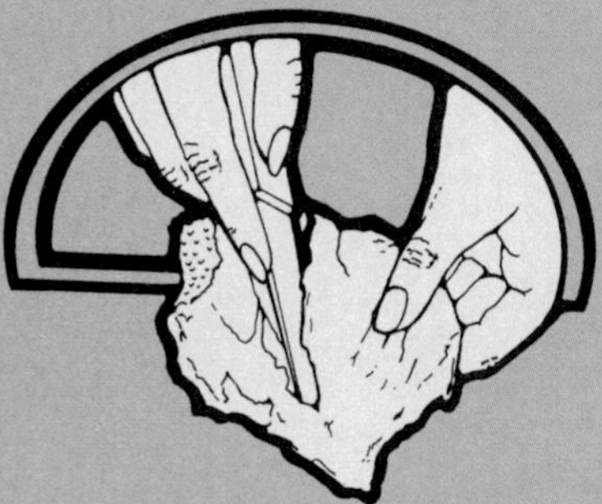

—Continue cutting, using a sawing motion. Press flat side of knife blade against rib bones. As you cut, gently pull meat up and away from bones, as shown.

Chicken with Pineapple

Pictured on pages 10 and 11—

- 1 2½- to 3-pound broiler-fryer chicken, cut up
- 2 tablespoons cooking oil *or* shortening
- 1 teaspoon salt
- 1 cup finely chopped onion
- 1 small green pepper, cut into thin strips
- 1 clove garlic, minced
- 2 medium tomatoes, peeled and coarsely chopped (1 cup)
- ¼ cup raisins (optional)
- 2 tablespoons lemon *or* lime juice
- ½ teaspoon dried oregano, crushed
- 1 8¼-ounce can pineapple chunks
- 2 tablespoons cold water
- 1 tablespoon cornstarch

In large skillet brown chicken in hot oil or shortening about 15 minutes, turning as necessary to brown evenly. Season with the salt and ⅛ teaspoon *pepper*. Remove chicken. In skillet drippings cook onion, green pepper, and garlic till onion is tender. Stir in tomatoes, raisins, lemon or lime juice, and oregano. Return chicken to skillet, placing meaty pieces toward center and remaining pieces around edge. Cover; simmer for 30 minutes. Add *undrained* pineapple. Simmer, uncovered, about 5 minutes more, or till chicken is tender.

Arrange chicken on heated serving platter. Remove fruit and vegetables from pan juices with slotted spoon and place on platter with chicken; cover and keep warm.

To make sauce, skim excess fat from pan juices. Blend together cold water and cornstarch; add to juices. Cook and stir till thickened and bubbly. Spoon sauce over chicken. Makes 4 servings.

Saucy Chicken Delight

- 1 teaspoon salt
- 1 teaspoon paprika
- Dash pepper
- 1 2½- to 3-pound broiler-fryer chicken, cut up
- 2 tablespoons cooking oil *or* shortening
- 1 10¾-ounce can condensed cream of chicken soup
- 1 8-ounce can tomato sauce
- 1 4-ounce can mushroom stems and pieces
- 1 teaspoon worcestershire sauce
- ½ teaspoon sugar
- ¼ teaspoon salt
- ½ cup dairy sour cream
- 1 teaspoon flour
- Hot cooked noodles

Combine 1 teaspoon salt, paprika, and pepper. Sprinkle mixture evenly over chicken pieces.

In a 12-inch skillet heat oil or shortening. Place meaty chicken pieces toward center and remaining pieces around edge. Brown over medium heat about 15 minutes, turning chicken as necessary to brown evenly. Place chicken in 13x9x2-inch baking pan.

In mixing bowl combine chicken soup, tomato sauce, *undrained* mushrooms, worcestershire sauce, sugar, and the ¼ teaspoon salt. Pour mixture over chicken. Cover pan with foil. Bake in 350° oven about 45 minutes or till chicken is tender. Remove chicken to heated serving platter; keep warm.

For sauce, in small saucepan blend sour cream and flour. Gradually blend in the hot soup mixture. Cook and stir till thickened and bubbly. Serve sauce over chicken and hot cooked noodles. Makes 4 to 6 servings.

Chicken Skillet

This colorful combination of chicken and carrots is easy to prepare—

- ⅓ cup all-purpose flour
- 1 teaspoon salt
- 1 teaspoon paprika
- ¼ teaspoon poultry seasoning
- 1 2½- to 3-pound broiler-fryer chicken, cut up
- 2 tablespoons cooking oil *or* shortening
- 1 teaspoon sugar
- 2 teaspoons instant chicken bouillon granules
- 1½ cups hot water
- 2 medium carrots, sliced (1 cup)
- 1 medium onion, sliced (½ cup)
- 2 tablespoons snipped parsley
- 1 tablespoon lemon juice

In a paper or plastic bag combine flour, salt, paprika, and poultry seasoning. Add chicken pieces, a few at a time; shake to coat evenly. Reserve excess flour mixture.

In a 12-inch skillet heat cooking oil or shortening. Place meaty chicken pieces toward center and remaining pieces around edge. Brown over medium heat about 15 minutes, turning chicken as necessary to brown evenly. Remove chicken from skillet.

To make sauce, stir reserved flour mixture and sugar into pan drippings. Dissolve bouillon granules in hot water; stir into skillet. Cook and stir till thickened and bubbly. Add carrots, onion, parsley, and lemon juice. Arrange chicken pieces atop vegetable mixture. Cover; simmer for 40 to 45 minutes or till chicken and vegetables are tender. Transfer chicken to heated serving platter. Skim excess fat from sauce. Pass sauce with chicken. Makes 4 to 6 servings.

Harvest Chicken

Roast chicken is enhanced by an herb and vegetable stuffing—

- 1/2 cup shredded carrot
- 1/2 cup chopped celery
- 1/4 cup chopped onion
- 1/4 cup margarine *or* butter
- 1/2 teaspoon ground sage *or* poultry seasoning
- 1/4 teaspoon salt
- 1/8 teaspoon ground cinnamon
- Dash pepper
- 4 cups dry white *or* whole wheat bread cubes (about 6 slices bread)
- 1 cup finely chopped, peeled apple (1 medium)
- 1/4 cup chopped walnuts (optional)
- 1/4 to 1/2 cup chicken broth
- 1 4- to 5-pound whole roasting chicken
- Cooking oil, melted margarine *or* butter
- Apple wedges *or* parsley sprig (optional)

To prepare stuffing, in skillet cook carrot, celery, and onion in margarine or butter till tender but not brown. Stir in sage or poultry seasoning, salt, cinnamon, and pepper. In a large mixing bowl combine bread cubes, chopped apple, and walnuts, if desired. Add cooked vegetable mixture. Drizzle with enough chicken broth to moisten. Toss lightly to mix.

Spoon some stuffing into neck cavity of chicken; skewer neck skin to back. Lightly spoon remaining stuffing into body cavity. (Bake any additional stuffing in a small covered casserole the last 20 to 30 minutes of roasting.) Tie legs securely to tail. Twist wing tips under back.

Place chicken, breast side up, on a rack in shallow roasting pan. Brush skin of bird with cooking oil or the melted margarine or butter. Roast, uncovered, in 375° oven for 2 to 2 1/2 hours or till drumstick moves easily in socket. Brush dry areas of skin occasionally with pan drippings, cooking oil, or melted margarine. Garnish with apple wedges or parsley, if desired. Makes 8 servings.

Chicken-Broccoli Crepes

Also pictured on the cover—

- 1 10-ounce package frozen cut broccoli
- 2 tablespoons margarine *or* butter
- 2 tablespoons all-purpose flour
- 1/4 teaspoon salt
- 1/4 teaspoon ground nutmeg
- 1 1/2 cups *reconstituted* nonfat dry milk *or* milk
- 3/4 cup shredded Swiss cheese (3 ounces)
- 2 cups finely chopped cooked chicken
- 12 Basic Crepes (see recipe, page 74)
- Paprika (optional)

Cook broccoli according to package directions; drain and set aside. For sauce, in medium saucepan melt margarine or butter; blend in flour, salt, and nutmeg. Add milk all at once. Cook and stir till thickened and bubbly. Cook, stirring constantly, for 2 minutes more. Add Swiss cheese; stir till melted. Set aside.

For filling combine chicken, broccoli, and *1 cup* of the cheese sauce. Spoon about 1/4 *cup* filling along center of *unbrowned* side of *each* crepe. Roll up crepes; place, seam side up, in 12x7 1/2x2-inch baking dish. Pour remaining cheese sauce over crepes. Sprinkle with paprika, if desired. Cover; bake in 375° oven for 18 to 20 minutes or till heated through. Serve immediately. Makes 6 servings.

Fruited Chicken

- 1/2 cup chopped celery
- 1/4 cup chopped onion
- 1/4 cup margarine *or* butter
- 3 cups dry bread cubes
- 1 cup chopped peeled apple
- 1 beaten egg
- 3/4 teaspoon poultry seasoning
- 1/2 teaspoon salt
- 1/2 of a 6-ounce can (1/3 cup) frozen orange juice concentrate
- 1 4- to 5-pound whole roasting chicken
- Cooking oil
- 1 8-ounce can whole cranberry sauce
- 1/4 cup light corn syrup

Cook celery and onion in *half* of the margarine or butter till tender. Add bread cubes, apple, egg, poultry seasoning, salt, and 1/8 teaspoon *pepper*. Stir in *3 tablespoons* of the orange juice concentrate; toss till all is moistened.

Rub neck and body cavities of chicken with salt; stuff loosely with bread mixture. Skewer neck to back. Tie legs securely to tail. Twist wing tips under back. Place chicken, breast side up, on a rack in shallow roasting pan. Brush skin with cooking oil. Cover loosely with foil; roast in 375° oven for 1 hour.

Meanwhile, prepare glaze. In small saucepan combine cranberry sauce, corn syrup, the remaining margarine or butter, and the remaining orange juice concentrate. Heat through; set aside.

Uncover chicken; continue roasting for 1 to 1 1/2 hours more or till done, basting with glaze last 30 minutes of roasting. Place chicken on serving platter. Garnish with celery leaves, if desired. Makes 8 servings.

Feature *Fruited Chicken* or *Chicken-Broccoli Crepes* for that extra touch of dining elegance. ▶

Oven Chicken with Vegetables

1 teaspoon salt
1 teaspoon onion powder
1 teaspoon poultry seasoning
½ teaspoon garlic powder
¼ teaspoon pepper
1 4- to 5-pound whole roasting chicken
4 to 6 medium potatoes, peeled and quartered
3 medium carrots, quartered
1 large onion, thinly sliced
½ cup water

In small bowl combine salt, onion powder, poultry seasoning, garlic powder, and pepper. Rub chicken with some of the seasoning mixture. Rub cavity of chicken with additional salt. Skewer neck skin to back. Tie legs to tail; twist wing tips under back. Place chicken in roasting pan or Dutch oven. Arrange potatoes, carrots, and onion around chicken. Add the ½ cup water and sprinkle with remaining seasoning mixture. Cover pan with foil or lid. Bake in 350° oven about 1¾ hours or till chicken and vegetables are tender. Skim off excess fat and pass juices. Makes 6 to 8 servings.

Cheesy Oven-Fried Chicken

Parmesan cheese and herbs season this crisp coating—

3 slices white bread, dried
½ cup grated parmesan cheese
1 teaspoon salt
½ teaspoon onion powder
¼ teaspoon dried thyme, crushed
⅛ teaspoon garlic powder
Dash pepper
1 2½- to 3-pound broiler-fryer chicken, cut up
¼ cup margarine *or* butter, melted

Coarsely crush dried bread. Combine crushed bread, parmesan cheese, salt, onion powder, thyme, garlic powder, and pepper. Dip chicken pieces in melted margarine or butter; roll in cheese mixture to coat. Place chicken pieces, skin side up and not touching, in greased large shallow baking pan. Bake in 375° oven 40 to 60 minutes or till chicken is tender. Do not turn. Makes 4 to 6 servings.

Oven Peach-Glazed Chicken

1 2½- to 3-pound broiler-fryer chicken, cut up
Salt
Paprika
1 16-ounce can peach slices
2 tablespoons lemon juice
1 tablespoon soy sauce
3 tablespoons margarine *or* butter
2 tablespoons cold water
4 teaspoons cornstarch
Hot cooked rice

Arrange chicken pieces in a single layer in a 13x9x2-inch pan. Sprinkle chicken with salt and paprika. Drain peaches, reserving ½ cup liquid. Combine reserved peach liquid, lemon juice, and soy sauce. Mash enough of the peach slices to make ½ cup. Coarsely chop remaining peach slices; set aside. Combine mashed peaches and the soy sauce mixture; drizzle over chicken. Dot with margarine or butter. Bake in 375° oven for 50 to 60 minutes or till done, basting occasionally with pan drippings. Remove chicken to heated platter; keep warm.

In small saucepan blend cold water and cornstarch. Add pan juices. Cook and stir till mixture is thickened and bubbly. Stir in reserved chopped peaches; heat through. Spoon sauce over chicken pieces and rice. Serves 4 to 6.

Chicken and Dumpling Stew

You'll look forward to sitting down to this rich, homey chicken stew—

1 2½- to 3-pound broiler-fryer chicken, cut up
4 cups water
3 medium onions, chopped (1½ cups)
2 teaspoons salt
½ teaspoon ground allspice
1 cup all-purpose flour
2 teaspoons baking powder
½ teaspoon salt
½ cup *reconstituted* nonfat dry milk *or* milk
2 tablespoons cooking oil *or* melted shortening
¾ cup cold water
⅓ cup all-purpose flour
1 16-ounce can mixed vegetables, drained

In Dutch oven or kettle place chicken pieces. Add the 4 cups water, chopped onions, the 2 teaspoons salt, and the allspice. Bring chicken mixture to boiling. Reduce heat; cover and simmer for 35 to 45 minutes or till chicken is nearly tender. Skim excess fat from liquid.

Meanwhile, for dumplings, in mixing bowl stir together the 1 cup flour, baking powder, and the ½ teaspoon salt. Combine the milk and cooking oil or melted shortening; add milk mixture all at once to dry ingredients, stirring just till moistened.

Blend the ¾ cup cold water and the ⅓ cup flour; stir into chicken mixture. Cook, stirring gently, till thickened and bubbly. Stir in mixed vegetables. Drop dumpling dough from tablespoon to make 8 mounds atop bubbling stew. Cover; simmer 15 minutes (do not lift cover). Makes 6 servings.

Chicken-Peanut Stew

- 1 2½ to 3-pound broiler-fryer chicken, cut up
- 2 tablespoons cooking oil
- 4 medium carrots, sliced
- 1 10-ounce package frozen cut green beans *or* one 16-ounce can green beans, drained
- 1 cup chopped onion
- 1 6-ounce can tomato paste
- ½ cup peanut butter
- 1 small bay leaf
- 2 teaspoons instant chicken bouillon granules
- 1 teaspoon chili powder
- Hot cooked rice

Halve chicken back and quarter the breast. In 12-inch skillet place meaty chicken pieces toward center and remaining pieces around edge. Brown chicken in hot oil about 10 minutes on each side; drain off fat. Add carrots, beans, and onion. Combine tomato paste, peanut butter, bay leaf, bouillon granules, chili powder, and ½ teaspoon *salt*; blend in 1¾ cups *water*. Pour over chicken and vegetables. Cover; simmer 25 to 30 minutes or till chicken is done and vegetables are tender. Remove bay leaf; discard. Spoon off fat. Serve over rice. Serves 6.

Oven Chicken Fricassee

- 3 tablespoons all-purpose flour
- 1 teaspoon paprika
- 1 2½- to 3-pound broiler-fryer chicken, cut up
- 1 10¾-ounce can condensed cream of mushroom soup
- 1 5⅓-ounce can (⅔ cup) evaporated milk
- ¼ cup finely chopped onion
- ½ teaspoon dried marjoram, crushed
- Snipped parsley (optional)

In shallow pan combine flour and paprika. Roll chicken in flour mixture to coat. Arrange chicken in 12x7½x2-inch baking dish. Bake, uncovered, in 375° oven for 30 minutes. Drain off excess fat.

Meanwhile, in saucepan combine mushroom soup, evaporated milk, chopped onion, and marjoram; cook and stir till heated through. Pour mixture over chicken. Cover baking dish with foil. Return to oven and bake about 30 minutes more or till chicken is tender. Garnish with parsley, if desired. Makes 4 servings.

Oven-Barbecued Chicken

- 2 2½- to 3-pound broiler-fryer chickens, cut up
- ½ cup catsup
- ⅓ cup vinegar
- ¼ cup packed brown sugar
- 2 tablespoons margarine *or* butter
- 2 tablespoons worcestershire sauce
- 2 tablespoons lemon juice
- 2 teaspoons salt
- 2 teaspoons chili powder
- 2 teaspoons prepared mustard
- 2 medium onions, sliced and separated into rings

Arrange chicken pieces in a 15x10x1-inch baking pan. Bake in a 375° oven for 40 minutes; drain off excess fat.

Meanwhile, for barbecue sauce, in saucepan combine catsup, vinegar, brown sugar, margarine or butter, worcestershire, lemon juice, salt, chili powder, and mustard. Stir in onions. Bring to boiling; reduce heat. Simmer, uncovered, for 10 minutes. Spoon some sauce over chicken; continue baking 10 minutes more. Turn chicken pieces; baste with remaining sauce. Bake 10 minutes more or till tender. Makes 8 to 10 servings.

Sunshine Chicken

- ¼ cup all-purpose flour
- ½ teaspoon salt
- ⅛ teaspoon ground cinnamon
- ⅛ teaspoon ground cloves
- Dash garlic powder
- 1 2½- to 3-pound broiler-fryer chicken, cut up
- 2 tablespoons cooking oil *or* shortening
- 1 6-ounce can frozen orange juice concentrate, thawed
- 1 juice can (¾ cup) water
- 1 tablespoon minced dried onion
- ¼ cup cold water
- 1 tablespoon all-purpose flour
- ½ teaspoon salt
- Hot cooked rice
- Snipped parsley (optional)

In a paper or plastic bag combine ¼ cup flour, ½ teaspoon salt, the cinnamon, cloves, and garlic powder. Add chicken pieces a few at a time; shake to coat pieces evenly.

In a 12-inch skillet heat oil or shortening. Place meaty chicken pieces toward center and remaining pieces around edge. Brown over medium heat 15 to 20 minutes, turning chicken as necessary to brown evenly.

In small mixing bowl combine orange juice concentrate, the juice can of water, and minced dried onion; pour over chicken in skillet. Cover and simmer about 30 minutes or till chicken is tender; turn occasionally to glaze. Remove chicken to heated serving platter; keep warm.

Blend together the ¼ cup cold water, the 1 tablespoon flour, and the ½ teaspoon salt; stir into orange juice mixture in skillet. Cook and stir till thickened and bubbly. Spoon orange sauce over chicken and hot cooked rice. Sprinkle with snipped parsley, if desired. Makes 4 to 6 servings.

Chicken Pot Pies

- 1/4 cup chopped onion
- 1/4 cup margarine *or* butter
- 1/4 cup all-purpose flour
- 2 teaspoons instant chicken bouillon granules
- 1/2 teaspoon salt
- 1/4 teaspoon dried thyme, crushed
- 1/4 teaspoon ground sage
- Dash pepper
- 1 1/3 cups *reconstituted* nonfat dry milk *or* milk
- 1 cup water
- 2 cups cubed cooked chicken *or* turkey
- 1 10-ounce package frozen mixed vegetables, cooked and drained *or* one 16-ounce can mixed vegetables, drained
- 2 tablespoons snipped parsley
- 1 cup Homemade Biscuit Mix (see recipe, page 73) *or* packaged biscuit mix
- 1/2 cup shredded American cheese *or* process cheese spread (2 ounces)
- 1/4 cup *reconstituted* nonfat dry milk *or* milk

Cook onion in margarine or butter till onion is tender but not brown. Blend in flour, chicken bouillon granules, salt, thyme, sage, and pepper. Add 1 1/3 cups milk and the water. Cook and stir till thickened and bubbly. Stir in cubed chicken or turkey, mixed vegetables, and parsley. Cook and stir till thickened and bubbly.

Meanwhile, for biscuit topper, combine Homemade Biscuit Mix or packaged biscuit mix and shredded cheese. Blend in 1/4 cup milk. Pour chicken mixture into five or six 10-ounce casseroles or one 1 1/2-quart casserole. Drop biscuit batter by tablespoons atop *hot* filling in casseroles. Bake in 400° oven for 15 to 20 minutes or till biscuits are lightly browned. Makes 5 or 6 servings.

Chicken Hoppin' John

- 2 slices bacon
- 1 2 1/2- to 3-pound broiler-fryer chicken, cut up
- 3/4 cup medium grain rice
- 1/2 cup chopped onion
- 1 tablespoon instant chicken bouillon granules
- Several dashes bottled hot pepper sauce
- 1 15-ounce can black-eyed peas, drained
- 1/4 cup snipped parsley
- 1/2 teaspoon dried thyme, crushed

In large skillet cook bacon till crisp. Drain, reserving 2 tablespoons drippings in skillet. Crumble bacon; set aside. Brown chicken slowly in bacon drippings. Season with 1/2 teaspoon *salt* and 1/8 teaspoon *pepper*. Cover; simmer 15 minutes. Add rice and onion. Dissolve bouillon granules in 2 cups *hot water*; add hot pepper sauce. Add to chicken. Combine black-eyed peas, parsley, and thyme; add to chicken; mix well. Cover; simmer 25 to 30 minutes or till chicken and rice are done. Garnish with crumbled bacon. Makes 4 to 6 servings.

Saucy Chicken Livers with Bacon

- 3 slices bacon
- 1 pound chicken livers, cut up
- 1/2 cup chopped onion
- 1 4-ounce can mushroom stems and pieces, drained
- 1/4 teaspoon dried thyme, crushed
- 1 teaspoon instant chicken bouillon granules
- 1 cup dairy sour cream
- 2 tablespoons all-purpose flour
- Hot cooked noodles

Cook bacon till crisp. Remove bacon, reserving drippings in skillet. Crumble bacon; set aside. Cook livers and onion in drippings 4 to 5 minutes or till livers are just slightly pink in center. Remove from heat. Stir in mushrooms, thyme, 1/4 teaspoon *salt*, and 1/8 teaspoon *pepper*. Dissolve bouillon granules in 1 cup *hot water*. Combine sour cream and flour; gradually blend in bouillon mixture. Add to liver mixture in skillet. Cook and stir till thickened; *do not boil*. Add bacon. Serve over noodles. Serves 4.

Tangy Chicken Bowl

You can use the blender to make this dressing, too—

- 1 8-ounce can kidney beans, drained
- 1 cup cooked chicken *or* turkey cut into strips
- 2 ounces American *or* cheddar cheese *or* process cheese spread, cut into strips
- 1/2 of a small cucumber, sliced
- 1/2 cup sliced celery
- 1/4 cup vinegar
- 3 tablespoons sugar
- 1 teaspoon grated onion
- 1/4 teaspoon salt
- 1/4 teaspoon celery seed
- 1/4 teaspoon dry mustard
- 1/8 teaspoon paprika
- 1/2 cup salad oil
- 4 cups torn salad greens
- 1 large tomato, cut into wedges

Combine beans, chicken, cheese, cucumber, and celery; chill. In mixer bowl combine next 7 ingredients. Gradually add oil, beating constantly. Chill. Toss greens with bean mixture. Shake dressing. Pour some over salad; toss. Pass remaining. Garnish with tomato. Serves 6.

Tangy Chicken Bowl makes a refreshing main dish meal. ▶

Special Turkey Croquettes

- ½ pound chicken livers
- 1 tablespoon margarine *or* butter
- 3 tablespoons margarine *or* butter
- ¼ cup all-purpose flour
- ½ teaspoon salt
- ¾ cup *reconstituted* nonfat dry milk *or* milk
- 1 cup ground cooked turkey *or* chicken
- ⅓ cup finely chopped celery
- ¼ cup finely chopped onion
- 2 cups crushed herb-seasoned stuffing mix
- 1 egg
- 2 tablespoons water
- Cooking oil *or* shortening for deep-fat frying

In covered saucepan cook chicken livers in the 1 tablespoon margarine or butter till no longer pink; stir occasionally. Drain chicken livers; grind chicken livers, using coarse blade of food grinder. Set aside.

In saucepan melt the remaining margarine or butter; blend in flour and salt. Add milk all at once. Cook and stir till thickened and bubbly. Remove from heat. Stir in ½ *cup* of the stuffing mix, ground chicken livers, ground turkey or chicken, celery, and onion; mix well. Chill mixture thoroughly.

Shape mixture into 12 balls. Roll balls in the remaining stuffing mix. Shape balls into cones, handling lightly. Beat together egg and water. Dip cones into egg mixture, then in stuffing mix again. Fry 2 or 3 croquettes in deep hot fat (365°) for 1 to 1½ minutes or till golden. Drain on paper toweling. Keep hot in warm oven while frying remaining. Makes 6 servings.

Turkey with Corn Stuffing

For a whole turkey, plan about 1 serving per pound—

- ½ cup chopped onion
- ½ cup finely shredded carrot
- ¼ cup margarine *or* butter
- 1 17-ounce can whole kernel corn
- 1 teaspoon poultry seasoning
- ½ teaspoon salt
- 10 cups dry bread cubes
- 1 12-pound turkey
- Cooking oil

Cook onion and carrot in margarine till tender. Drain corn; reserve and set aside liquid. Stir corn, poultry seasoning, salt, and ¼ teaspoon *pepper* into onion mixture.

In large bowl add corn mixture to bread cubes. Drizzle with enough of the corn liquid to moisten. Toss lightly to mix. Rinse turkey; pat dry. Rub cavities with salt. Spoon some stuffing into neck cavity; skewer neck skin to back. Lightly spoon remaining stuffing into body cavity. (Bake any remaining stuffing in covered casserole the last 30 to 40 minutes of roasting, adding additional water, if necessary.) Tuck drumsticks under band of skin at tail, or tie legs to tail. Twist wing tips under back.

Place turkey, breast side up, on a rack in shallow roasting pan. Brush with cooking oil. Insert meat thermometer in center of inside thigh muscle, making sure bulb does not touch bone. Cover turkey loosely with foil. Roast in 325° oven for a total of 4½ to 5 hours. After about 3 hours (when turkey is ⅔ done), cut band of skin or string between legs. About 45 minutes before turkey is done, remove foil. Turkey is done when thermometer registers 185° and drumstick moves easily in socket. Let stand 15 minutes before carving. Makes 12 to 16 servings.

Sweet-Sour Turkey Drumsticks

- ½ cup chopped onion
- 2 tablespoons cooking oil
- ¼ cup honey
- ¼ cup vinegar
- 1½ teaspoons worcestershire sauce
- ½ teaspoon ground allspice
- ¼ teaspoon salt
- Dash pepper
- 2 turkey legs (about 2 pounds total)
- 1 teaspoon instant chicken bouillon granules
- ½ cup hot water
- ½ cup cold water
- 2 tablespoons all-purpose flour
- Hot cooked noodles *or* rice (optional)

In small saucepan cook onion in cooking oil. Remove from heat; stir in honey, vinegar, worcestershire sauce, allspice, salt, and pepper. Place turkey legs in shallow dish; pour honey mixture over. Cover and refrigerate several hours or overnight. Drain drumsticks, reserving marinade. Place turkey legs in a 12x7½x2-inch baking dish or 13x9x2-inch baking pan. Dissolve bouillon granules in the ½ cup hot water; stir into reserved marinade. Pour over turkey legs. Cover pan with foil; bake in 325° oven about 1½ to 2 hours or till tender.

Remove turkey legs to heated serving platter; keep warm. For gravy, transfer pan juices to saucepan. Blend the ½ cup cold water and the flour; stir into pan juices. Cook and stir till thickened and bubbly; pass gravy with turkey legs. Serve over noodles or rice, if desired. Makes 4 servings.

Turkey Frame-Bean Soup

Make good use of every bit of meat on a turkey frame with this hearty soup—

- 1 cup dry navy beans
- 8 cups water
- 2 teaspoons salt
- 1 meaty turkey frame
- 1 medium onion, chopped
- 1½ teaspoons worcestershire sauce
- ½ teaspoon poultry seasoning *or* ground sage
- ⅛ teaspoon pepper
- 1 17-ounce can whole kernel corn, drained
- 2 stalks celery, sliced (1 cup)
- 2 medium carrots, sliced (1 cup)
- 1 medium turnip, chopped (1 cup)
- French bread slices *or* rolls (optional)

Rinse navy beans. In 5-quart Dutch oven combine beans, the water, and salt. Bring to boiling; reduce heat and simmer for 2 minutes. Remove from heat. Cover; let stand for 1 hour. (Or, soak beans in the water overnight in a covered pan.) *Do not drain*.

Break turkey frame to fit Dutch oven. Add to navy bean mixture. Stir in chopped onion, worcestershire sauce, poultry seasoning or sage, and pepper. Cover and simmer for 1 hour.

Remove turkey frame; cool slightly. Cut meat off frame; chop meat. Slightly mash beans. Return chopped meat to Dutch oven. Add drained corn, sliced celery, sliced carrots, and chopped turnip. Cover and simmer about 30 minutes more or till vegetables are tender. Serve with thick slices of French bread or rolls, if desired. Makes 8 to 10 servings.

Curried Turkeywiches

- 1½ cups chopped cooked turkey *or* chicken
- ½ cup chopped, peeled apple
- ⅓ cup finely chopped celery
- 2 tablespoons finely chopped onion
- 2 tablespoons snipped parsley
- ½ cup salad dressing *or* mayonnaise
- 1 to 1½ teaspoons curry powder
- 6 slices white bread, toasted
- Margarine *or* butter

Combine turkey or chicken, apple, celery, onion, and parsley. Combine salad dressing or mayonnaise, curry powder, ¼ teaspoon *salt*, and dash *pepper*; stir into turkey mixture. Spread one side of each toast slice with margarine or butter. Arrange on baking sheet, margarine side up; divide and spoon turkey mixture over toast. Broil 4 to 6 inches from heat for 4 to 5 minutes or till heated through. Sprinkle with paprika, if desired. Makes 6 servings.

Turkey Casserole

- 2 tablespoons margarine *or* butter
- 2 tablespoons all-purpose flour
- 1 teaspoon instant chicken bouillon granules
- 2 cups chopped cooked turkey *or* chicken
- 1 10-ounce package frozen mixed vegetables, cooked and drained, *or* one 16-ounce can mixed vegetables, drained
- ¾ cup shredded American cheese *or* process cheese spread (3 ounces)
- ½ cup soft bread crumbs
- 1 tablespoon margarine *or* butter, melted

In saucepan melt 2 tablespoons margarine or butter; blend in flour. Stir in bouillon granules and 1 cup *water*; cook and stir till mixture is thickened and bubbly. Remove from heat; stir in turkey or chicken, mixed vegetables, and shredded American cheese or process cheese spread. Turn into a 1-quart casserole. Combine crumbs and 1 tablespoon melted margarine or butter; sprinkle over casserole. Bake in 350° oven 30 to 35 minutes or till heated through. Makes 4 or 5 servings.

Turkey Creole

- ½ cup chopped green papper
- ½ cup chopped celery
- ¼ cup chopped onion
- 1 tablespoon margarine *or* butter
- 1 tablespoon all-purpose flour
- 1 16-ounce can tomatoes, cut up
- 1 8-ounce can tomato sauce
- 1 teaspoon sugar
- ½ teaspoon salt
- ½ teaspoon dried thyme, crushed
- ¼ teaspoon garlic powder
- 1 bay leaf
- Several dashes bottled hot pepper sauce
- Dash pepper
- 2 cups chopped cooked turkey *or* chicken
- Hot cooked rice

Cook green pepper, celery, and onion in margarine or butter till tender but not brown. Stir in flour. Stir in *undrained* tomatoes, tomato sauce, sugar, salt, thyme, garlic powder, bay leaf, hot pepper sauce, and pepper. Cook and stir till thickened and bubbly. Stir in chopped turkey or chicken. Cover and simmer for 5 to 10 minutes. Remove bay leaf; discard. Serve over hot cooked rice. Makes 4 or 5 servings.

Fish & Seafood

Fish frequently costs less per serving than the more commonly purchased red meats because there is little waste from bone or fat.

Using Frozen Fish

Frozen fish is available year round in most markets. It may be purchased whole or cut into steaks, fillets, or chunks. You can substitute frozen fish for fresh fish in recipe preparation if the frozen fish is thawed just before using or if extra cooking time is allowed. Use thawed fish immediately, and do not refreeze. Fish sticks or individual breaded portions should not be thawed before cooking.

Buying Fresh Fish

Purchase the variety of fresh fish that is in season for the best price. Fish marketers can guide you both in determining seasonal availabilities and in choosing the fish that will best suit your family needs and budget. Many fresh fish are seasonal delicacies. But available all year round are fresh rock bass, carp, cod, flounder, haddock, halibut, perch, red snapper, salmon, sole, and tuna.

Fortunately, different varieties of fish can be successfully substituted in recipes for one another. So, choose the variety and the form of fish according to how well it fits

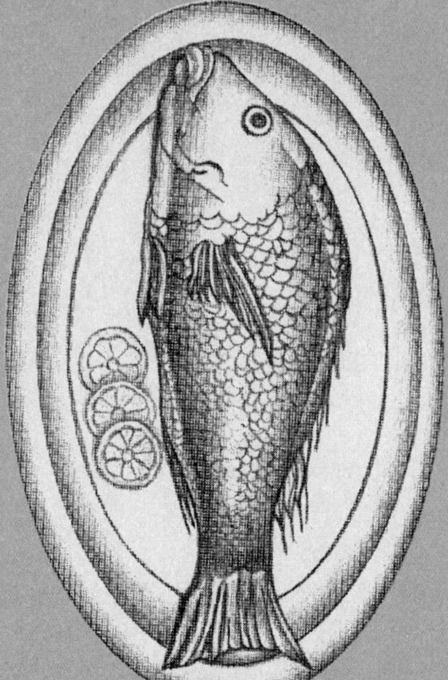

into your budget. When shopping, keep in mind that some of the lesser-known varieties may cost less than the well-known varieties.

Fish Sticks

Fish sticks can be economical, as there is no waste from bone or fat. Look at the list of ingredients on packages of breaded or batter-coated fish sticks to determine which gives the most fish for your money.

Fish not only is a money saver, but also is highly nutritional. Fish is a good source of high-quality protein, niacin, iodine, and magnesium. It also contributes to the iron and calcium you need. And fish is generally low in fat, cholesterol, and calories.

To help you in meal planning and fish buying, allow about 4 servings per pound from fresh or frozen fish fillets, steaks, portions, and fish sticks. Canned fish yields 6 servings per pound.

Canned Tuna and Salmon

Canned tuna and salmon share the advantage of long shelf lives. Varieties and styles count here when you're counting pennies.

Tuna prices are determined by the type of tuna and the pack. Choose the canned tuna that best fits your needs. "White" or "white albacore" is more costly than

"light" tuna. The fancy or solid-pack style commands the highest price since it uses large, whole pieces of tuna. Cheaper styles, in order of descending costs, are chunk, flaked, and grated.

The price of canned salmon is determined by the type of salmon. When buying salmon remember this rule of thumb: the redder the flesh, the higher the price. Salmon varieties from pinkest (least expensive) to reddest (most expensive) are chum, pink, silver, king, chinook, and sockeye.

Seaside Manicotti

- 6 manicotti shells
- 1 10-ounce package frozen chopped spinach
- ½ cup chopped onion
- 1 clove garlic, minced
- 2 tablespooons margarine *or* butter
- 3 tablespoons all-purpose flour
- 2 cups *reconstituted* nonfat dry milk *or* milk
- 1 cup shredded Swiss cheese (4 ounces)
- ¼ cup grated parmesan cheese
- 2 tablespoons margarine *or* butter, melted
- ½ teaspoon salt
- 1 pound fresh *or* frozen perch fillets *or* other fish fillets, cooked and flaked
- Ground nutmeg

Cook manicotti in boiling salted water according to package directions; drain. Cook spinach according to package directions; drain well, pressing out excess liquid.

Meanwhile, prepare cheese sauce. In saucepan cook onion and garlic in the 2 tablespooons margarine or butter till tender but not brown. Blend in flour. Add milk all at once; cook and stir till thickened and bubbly. Stir in Swiss cheese till melted. Combine ½ *cup* of the sauce with the spinach, parmesan, the 2 tablespoons melted margarine or butter, and the salt. Fold in flaked fish. Stuff manicotti shells with fish mixture.

Pour *half* of the remaining sauce into a 1½-quart oval au gratin dish or 10x6x2-inch baking dish. Place manicotti in dish atop sauce. Pour remaining sauce over manicotti. Cover and bake in 350° oven for 30 to 35 minutes or till heated through. Sprinkle ground nutmeg over manicotti before serving, if desired. Makes 6 servings.

Lemon-Sauced Fish

- 1 pound fresh *or* frozen fish fillets
- 1 tablespoon margarine, melted
- 1 tablespoon finely chopped onion
- 1 tablespoon margarine
- 1½ teaspoons cornstarch
- 1 teaspoon instant chicken bouillon granules
- 1 tablespoon snipped parsley
- 2 teaspoons lemon juice
- Dash ground nutmeg

Thaw fish, if frozen. Separate fish into 4 serving-size pieces; arrange in single layer on greased unheated rack of broiler pan. Brush *half* the *melted* margarine over fish. Broil fish 4 inches from heat for 5 to 8 minutes; turn. Brush with remaining melted margarine. Broil 5 to 8 minutes more or till fish flakes easily.

Meanwhile, in saucepan cook onion in the 1 tablespoon margarine till tender but not brown. Blend in cornstarch. Add bouillon granules and ½ cup *water;* cook and stir till thickened. Add parsley, lemon juice, nutmeg, and dash *pepper;* heat through. Pour some sauce over fish; pass remaining. Serves 4.

Cheesy Fish Fillets

- 1 pound fresh *or* frozen fish fillets
- 2 tablespooons margarine *or* butter, melted
- 2 tablespoons catsup
- 1 tablespoon salad dressing *or* mayonnaise
- 2 teaspoons sweet pickle relish
- 1 teaspoon prepared mustard
- ¼ cup shredded American cheese *or* process cheese spread (1 ounce)

Thaw fish, if frozen. Separate into 4 serving-size pieces. Arrange fish in single layer on greased unheated rack of broiler pan or in a greased baking pan. Tuck under any thin edges. Brush *half* the melted margarine or butter over fish. Season with ½ teaspoon *salt* and dash *pepper*. Broil fish 4 inches from heat for 5 minutes; turn. Brush with remaining melted margarine or butter. Broil 5 to 8 minutes longer or till fish flakes easily when tested with a fork. Combine catsup, salad dressing or mayonnaise, pickle relish, and mustard; spoon atop fillets. Sprinkle with cheese. Broil 2 minutes more. Makes 4 servings.

Fillets Parmesan

- 1½ pounds fresh *or* frozen fish fillets
- 1 cup plain yogurt
- 2 tablespoons all-purpose flour
- 1 10¾-ounce can condensed golden mushroom soup
- ⅓ cup grated parmesan cheese
- 1 teaspoon lemon juice
- ½ teaspoon dried basil, crushed
- Snipped parsley
- Grated parmesan cheese
- Hot cooked rice

Thaw fish, if frozen. Cut into 6 serving-size pieces. Place in 12x7½x2-inch baking dish. In saucepan blend ¼ *cup* of the yogurt and the flour. Stir in remaining yogurt, the soup, the ⅓ cup parmesan, the lemon juice, and basil. Cook and stir over medium heat till thickened; *do not boil.* Pour soup mixture over fillets. Bake in 350° oven for 20 to 25 minutes or till fish flakes easily when tested with a fork. Sprinkle with parsley and additional parmesan cheese; serve with hot cooked rice. Makes 6 servings.

Shrimp Crepes Parmesan

- 1/3 cup chopped green pepper
- 1/4 cup finely chopped onion
- 3 tablespoons margarine *or* butter
- 2 tablespoons all-purpose flour
- 1 teaspoon instant chicken bouillon granules
- 1 13-ounce can (1 2/3 cups) evaporated milk
- 1/2 cup *reconstituted* nonfat dry milk *or* milk
- 1/3 cup grated parmesan cheese
- 1 teaspoon lemon juice
- 1/2 teaspoon worcestershire sauce
- 1 8-ounce can water chestnuts, drained and sliced
- 1 4 1/2-ounce can shrimp, drained and halved lengthwise
- 2 hard-cooked eggs, chopped
- 12 Basic Crepes (see recipe, page 74)
- Snipped parsley

In saucepan cook green pepper and onion in margarine till vegetables are tender but not brown. Blend in flour and bouillon granules. Add evaporated milk and milk all at once. Cook and stir till thickened and bubbly. Remove from heat. Add parmesan cheese, lemon juice, and worcestershire; stir till cheese is melted. Set aside *1 cup* of the cheese mixture. Stir water chestnuts, shrimp, and hard-cooked eggs into remaining mixture.

Spoon *about 1/4 cup* of the shrimp mixture down center of unbrowned side of crepe; roll up. Place seam side down in 12x7 1/2x2-inch baking dish. Repeat with remaining crepes and shrimp mixture. Pour the reserved 1 cup cheese mixture over crepes. Cover; bake in 375° oven about 25 minutes or till heated through. Sprinkle with parsley. Makes 6 servings.

Curried Fish Fillets

Also pictured on the cover—

- 1 16-ounce package frozen fish fillets
- Salt
- Paprika
- 1/4 cup chopped celery
- 1/4 cup chopped onion
- 1 tablespoon cooking oil
- 1 1/2 cups dry bread cubes
- Dash ground ginger
- Dash pepper
- 1 7 1/2-ounce can tomatoes
- 2 tablespoons margarine *or* butter
- 4 teaspoons all-purpose flour
- 3/4 to 1 teaspoon curry powder
- 1/4 teaspoon salt
- 1 cup *reconstituted* nonfat dry milk *or* milk

Partially thaw block of fish (about 1 hour at room temperature). Cut fish block crosswise into 4 equal pieces. Place fish in 10x6x2-inch baking dish. Season with a little salt and paprika.

For stuffing, cook celery and onion in oil till crisp-tender. Combine bread cubes, ginger, and pepper. Add vegetable mixture. Drain and cut up tomatoes, reserving liquid. Toss tomatoes with bread mixture, adding enough of the reserved tomato liquid to moisten (about 1 to 2 tablespoons). Place *1/3 cup* stuffing atop each fish portion. Bake, uncovered, in 350° oven for 25 to 30 minutes or till fish flakes easily when tested with a fork.

Meanwhile, prepare curry sauce. In saucepan melt margarine or butter. Blend in flour, curry powder, and the 1/4 teaspoon salt. Add milk all at once. Cook and stir till thickened and bubbly. Spoon curry sauce over fish just before serving. Makes 4 servings.

Fish and Vegetable Chowder

- 1/2 pound fresh *or* frozen haddock fillets *or* other fish fillets
- 2 slices bacon
- 2 tablespoons margarine *or* butter
- 1/4 cup chopped celery
- 1/4 cup chopped onion
- 1/4 cup all-purpose flour
- 1 teaspoon instant chicken bouillon granules
- 1/2 teaspoon dried marjoram, crushed
- 1/4 teaspoon salt
- 3 cups *reconstituted* nonfat dry milk *or* milk
- 1/2 cup water
- 1 10-ounce package frozen mixed vegetables *or* one 16-ounce can mixed vegetables, drained
- 1 cup shredded American cheese *or* process cheese spread (4 ounces)

Thaw fish, if frozen. Cut fillets into 3/4-inch pieces. In saucepan cook bacon till crisp; drain, reserving drippings in pan. Crumble bacon and set aside. Add margarine or butter to bacon drippings; add chopped celery and onion and cook till vegetables are tender but not brown. Blend in flour, chicken bouillon granules, marjoram, and salt. Add milk and water all at once. Cook and stir till thickened and bubbly.

Stir in the mixed vegetables. Cover and simmer for 10 minutes. Add fish pieces and shredded cheese; cook about 5 minutes more or till fish flakes easily when tested with a fork and the cheese is melted. Garnish with crumbled bacon. Makes 4 servings.

Rich and colorful *Fish and Vegetable Chowder* and *Curried Fish Fillets* will tempt all fish-lovers. ▶

Mexican Tuna Casseroles

1 beaten egg
1/4 cup fine dry bread crumbs
1/4 cup finely chopped onion
1/4 cup catsup
1/2 teaspoon dry mustard
1/4 teaspoon salt
1 9 1/4-ounce can tuna, drained and flaked
1 cup all-purpose flour
1 cup yellow cornmeal
2 tablespoons sugar
4 teaspoons baking powder
1/2 teaspoon salt
1 cup *reconstituted* nonfat dry milk *or* milk
2 eggs
1/4 cup cooking oil *or* melted shortening
1 cup shredded American cheese *or* process cheese spread (4 ounces)
1 16-ounce can tomatoes, cut up
4 teaspoons cornstarch
1/2 cup finely chopped green pepper
1 teaspoon worcestershire sauce
1/2 teaspoon chili powder

In mixing bowl combine the 1 beaten egg, bread crumbs, onion, catsup, dry mustard, and the 1/4 teaspoon salt. Add tuna; mix well. Spread tuna mixture in six greased 8- or 10-ounce individual casseroles.

In another bowl stir together flour, cornmeal, sugar, baking powder, and 1/2 teaspoon salt. Add milk, 2 eggs, and oil or melted shortening. Beat with rotary beater about 1 minute or just till smooth. Stir in *half* of the shredded cheese. Pour atop tuna mixture in casseroles. Bake in 350° oven about 25 minutes or till golden brown.

Meanwhile, prepare sauce. In saucepan gradually stir *undrained* tomatoes into cornstarch. Add green pepper, worcestershire sauce, and chili powder. Cook and stir till thickened and bubbly.

Let casseroles stand for 5 minutes after removing from oven. Using a narrow spatula, loosen mixture from casseroles. Invert onto individual serving plates. Sprinkle remaining shredded cheese atop. Serve with sauce spooned over. Makes 6 servings.

Fish Sticks Polynesian

Try this economical sweet-sour casserole, pictured on pages 10 and 11—

1 8- to 10-ounce package frozen fish sticks
1 15 1/2-ounce can pineapple chunks
1 tablespoon cornstarch
1 tablespoon soy sauce
1 1/2 teaspoons instant chicken bouillon granules
2 tablespoons vinegar
1 1/2 cups cooked *or* leftover rice
1 10-ounce package frozen peas, thawed, *or* one 16-ounce can peas, drained
Carrot curls and parsley sprigs (optional)

Set aside 4 fish sticks; cut remaining into 1-inch pieces. Drain pineapple chunks, reserving 2/3 cup liquid. In saucepan gradually stir reserved liquid into cornstarch. Add soy sauce and chicken bouillon granules. Cook and stir till thickened and bubbly. Remove from heat; stir in vinegar.

Combine cooked rice, peas, pineapple chunks, and fish pieces. Stir sauce into fish and rice mixture; turn into 8x1 1/2-inch round baking dish. Arrange reserved whole fish sticks atop. Bake in 350° oven 30 to 35 minutes or till rice mixture is heated through. Garnish with carrot curls and parsley sprigs, if desired. Makes 4 servings.

Nicoise-Style Salad

This colorful salad boasts a vegetable combination with a tangy herb dressing—

1/3 cup salad oil
3 tablespoons lemon juice
2 tablespoons vinegar
1 teaspoon sugar
1 teaspoon dry mustard
3/4 teaspoon paprika
1/2 teaspoon salt
1/2 teaspoon dried basil, crushed
1 medium head lettuce, torn into pieces *or* 6 cups torn assorted salad greens
1 9 1/4-ounce can tuna, chilled and drained
1 10-ounce package frozen cut green beans, cooked, drained, and chilled, *or* one 16-ounce can cut green beans, drained and chilled*
2 medium potatoes, cooked, peeled, chilled, and cubed (2 cups)
2 medium tomatoes, peeled and cut into wedges
3 hard-cooked eggs, cut into wedges
1 small onion, thinly sliced and separated into rings

To make dressing, in screw-top jar combine salad oil, lemon juice, vinegar, sugar, dry mustard, paprika, salt, and basil. Cover and shake well to mix. Chill.

Just before serving arrange lettuce or salad greens in salad bowl. Break tuna into chunks; mound in center of torn lettuce. Arrange chilled green beans, potatoes, tomato wedges, egg wedges, and onion rings atop the lettuce. (Or, arrange in individual salad bowls.) Shake chilled dressing and drizzle over salad; toss lightly. Makes 6 servings.

**Note*: If using home-canned green beans, boil for 10 to 15 minutes; drain and chill.

Tuna Chowder

- 2 medium carrots, thinly sliced
- ½ cup chopped onion
- 3 tablespoons margarine
- 2 medium potatoes, peeled and cut into ½-inch cubes
- 1 16-ounce can tomatoes, cut up
- ½ of a 10-ounce package frozen peas
- ½ teaspoon dried thyme, crushed
- 1 10¾-ounce can condensed cream of celery soup
- 2½ cups *reconstituted* nonfat dry milk *or* milk
- 1 9¼-ounce can tuna, drained and broken into chunks

In large covered saucepan cook carrots and onion in margarine till onion is tender but not brown. Add potatoes, *undrained* tomatoes, peas, thyme, ½ cup *water*, ½ teaspoon *salt*, and ⅛ teaspoon *pepper*. Bring to boiling; reduce heat. Cover; simmer for 10 to 15 minutes or till vegetables are just tender. Add soup, milk, and tuna; heat through. Makes 6 servings.

Tuna-Apple Salad

- 3 cups shredded cabbage
- 1 6½-ounce can tuna, drained and flaked
- ¾ cup shredded American cheese *or* process cheese spread (3 ounces)
- ½ cup thinly sliced celery
- ⅔ cup salad dressing *or* mayonnaise
- 1 tablespoon *reconstituted* nonfat dry milk *or* milk
- 1 tablespoon lemon juice
- 1 tablespoon salad oil
- ½ teaspoon sugar
- ½ teaspoon dry mustard
- 2 medium apples, cored and chopped (2 cups)

Combine cabbage, tuna, shredded cheese, and celery; chill. Stir together salad dressing or mayonnaise, milk, lemon juice, oil, sugar, mustard, and ¼ teaspoon *salt*. Add chopped apples and chill. To serve, pour dressing mixture over tuna mixture; mix well. Serves 4.

Tuna with Pinwheel Biscuits

- ½ cup chopped celery
- 2 tablespoons chopped onion
- 1 cup Homemade Biscuit Mix (see recipe, page 73) *or* packaged biscuit mix
- ¼ cup *reconstituted* nonfat dry milk *or* milk
- ¾ cup shredded American cheese *or* process cheese spread (3 ounces)
- 1 10¾-ounce can condensed cream of celery soup
- 1 11-ounce can condensed cheddar cheese soup
- ½ cup *reconstituted* nonfat dry milk *or* milk
- 2 6½-ounce cans tuna, drained and broken into chunks
- 2 16-ounce cans mixed vegetables, drained

Cook celery and onion in boiling salted water till crisp-tender; drain. Meanwhile, to prepare pinwheel biscuits, combine biscuit mix and ¼ cup milk. Stir just till dough clings together. Turn out onto lightly floured surface; knead 5 strokes. Roll to 10x6-inch rectangle. Sprinkle with cheese. Roll up jelly roll-style, starting at narrow end; seal edge. Cut into twelve ½-inch slices. In saucepan combine soups, ½ cup milk, the tuna, mixed vegetables, and onion-celery mixture; bring to boiling. Pour into 12x7½x2-inch baking dish. Arrange biscuits, cut side down, atop *boiling* tuna mixture. Bake in 425° oven 15 to 20 minutes. Serves 6.

Tuna and Cheese Stuffed Manicotti

- 8 manicotti shells
- ⅓ cup finely chopped green pepper
- ¼ cup finely chopped onion
- 2 tablespoons margarine
- 2 beaten eggs
- 1 cup cream-style cottage cheese
- ¼ cup grated parmesan cheese
- ½ teaspoon dried marjoram, crushed
- 1 cup cooked peas, chopped broccoli, cauliflower, *or* carrots
- 1 6½-ounce can tuna, drained and flaked
- 3 tablespoons margarine
- 3 tablespoons all-purpose flour
- ¼ teaspoon salt
- Dash pepper
- 1½ cups *reconstituted* nonfat dry milk *or* milk
- 1 cup shredded American cheese *or* process cheese spread (4 ounces)
- ¼ cup grated parmesan cheese

Cook manicotti shells according to package directions; drain. Cook green pepper and onion in 2 tablespoons margarine till tender but not brown; set aside. Combine eggs, cottage cheese, ¼ cup parmesan cheese, and marjoram. Add choice of cooked vegetable, tuna, and green pepper-onion mixture; mix well. Spoon mixture into cooked manicotti shells. Arrange stuffed shells in a single layer in 12x7½x 2-inch baking dish.

In saucepan melt 3 tablespoons margarine. Blend in flour, salt, and pepper. Add milk all at once. Cook and stir till thickened and bubbly. Add shredded cheese, stirring to melt; pour over stuffed shells. Sprinkle with ¼ cup parmesan. Cover; bake in 350° oven 35 to 40 minutes or till heated through. Makes 8 servings.

Curried Salmon Soufflé

1 7¾-ounce can salmon *or* one 6½-ounce can tuna
Reconstituted nonfat dry milk *or* milk
2 tablespoons finely chopped onion
2 tablespoons finely chopped green pepper
¼ cup margarine *or* butter
¼ cup all-purpose flour
1 teaspoon curry powder
½ teaspoon salt
4 egg yolks
4 egg whites
⅓ cup chopped onion
2 tablespoons margarine *or* butter
2 tablespoons all-purpose flour
½ teaspoon instant chicken bouillon granules
½ cup *reconstituted* nonfat dry milk *or* milk
½ cup water
¼ teaspoon worcestershire sauce

Drain salmon, reserving liquid. Add enough milk to reserved salmon liquid to make *1 cup*. (If using tuna, drain. Use *1 cup milk* for liquid.) Set aside. In saucepan cook 2 tablespoons finely chopped onion and the green pepper in ¼ cup margarine or butter till tender but not brown. Blend in ¼ cup flour, curry powder, and ½ teaspoon salt. Add milk and salmon liquid mixture (or 1 cup milk) all at once. Cook and stir till thickened and bubbly. Remove from heat.

Beat egg yolks till thick and lemon-colored. *Slowly* add thickened milk mixture, stirring constantly. Stir in salmon or tuna. Beat egg whites till stiff peaks form. Fold salmon mixture into egg whites. Turn into 1½-quart soufflé dish or casserole with straight sides. Bake in 350° oven about 45 minutes or till knife inserted near center comes out clean. Serve the soufflé immediately.

Meanwhile, prepare sauce. In saucepan cook ⅓ cup onion in 2 tablespoons margarine or butter till tender. Blend in 2 tablespoons flour, bouillon granules, and ¼ teaspoon *salt*. Add ½ cup milk, the water, and worcestershire all at once. Cook and stir till thickened and bubbly. Serve over soufflé. Makes 4 servings.

Sour Cream-Topped Salmon Loaf

1 15½-ounce can salmon
2 beaten eggs
2¼ cups soft bread crumbs (3 slices)
2 tablespoons finely chopped onion
2 tablespoons snipped parsley
2 teaspoons lemon juice
¼ cup dairy sour cream
2 tablespoons *reconstituted* nonfat dry milk *or* milk
2 tablespoons salad dressing *or* mayonnaise
1 teaspoon finely chopped onion
¼ teaspoon dried dillweed
Dash salt
Few drops bottled hot pepper sauce

Drain and flake salmon, discarding skin and bones. In bowl combine eggs, bread crumbs, 2 tablespoons onion, parsley, lemon juice, ½ teaspoon *salt*, and ⅛ teaspoon *pepper*. Add salmon; mix well. Pat mixture into greased 7½x3½x2-inch loaf pan. Bake in 350° oven 35 to 40 minutes or till done.

For sauce, in small saucepan combine sour cream, milk, salad dressing or mayonnaise, 1 teaspoon chopped onion, dillweed, dash salt, and hot pepper sauce. Heat through; *do not boil*. Spoon some sauce atop salmon loaf; pass remaining sauce. Makes 4 to 6 servings.

Tuna and Garbanzo Stuffed Peppers

4 large green peppers *or* 4 large tomatoes
1 15-ounce can garbanzo beans, drained
1 6½-ounce can tuna, drained and flaked
½ cup shredded carrot
½ cup chopped celery
2 tablespoons finely chopped onion
½ teaspoon salt
¼ teaspoon dried oregano, crushed
½ cup salad dressing *or* mayonnaise
2 teaspoons prepared mustard
½ teaspoon worcestershire sauce
Shredded carrot (optional)
Lettuce (optional)

Cut peppers in half lengthwise; discard seeds and membranes. Cook peppers in boiling salted water about 3 minutes; drain and chill. (For tomatoes, place stem end down on cutting surface. With sharp knife cut tomato into 4 to 6 wedges, cutting to, but not through, the stem end of the tomato. Cover and chill.)

In mixing bowl combine garbanzo beans, tuna, ½ cup shredded carrot, chopped celery, chopped onion, salt, and oregano. For dressing, combine salad dressing or mayonnaise, prepared mustard, and worcestershire sauce. Pour dressing over tuna-garbanzo mixture; toss lightly. Chill.

To serve, sprinkle insides of green peppers or tomatoes with a little salt; spoon tuna-garbanzo mixture into peppers or tomatoes. If desired, garnish with additional shredded carrot. Serve on lettuce-lined plates, if desired. Makes 4 servings.

Cheesy Tuna-Spinach Casserole

The unusual crunch in this creamy casserole is from water chestnuts—

- 4 ounces medium noodles
- 1 10-ounce package frozen chopped spinach, thawed
- ½ cup chopped onion
- 3 tablespoons margarine *or* butter
- 3 tablespoons all-purpose flour
- ½ teaspoon dry mustard
- ¼ teaspoon salt
- 1½ cups *reconstituted* nonfat dry milk *or* milk
- 1 cup shredded American *or* Swiss cheese *or* process cheese spread (4 ounces)
- 1 6½-ounce can tuna, drained and flaked
- 1 8-ounce can water chestnuts, drained and sliced (optional)
- ⅓ cup fine dry bread crumbs
- 1 tablespoon margarine *or* butter, melted

Cook noodles according to package directions; drain. Meanwhile, press excess moisture from thawed spinach; set aside.

In saucepan cook chopped onion in the 3 tablespoons margarine or butter till tender but not brown. Blend in flour, dry mustard, and salt. Add milk all at once. Cook and stir till thickened and bubbly. Add shredded cheese; stir till melted. Stir in cooked noodles, thawed spinach, and tuna; stir in sliced water chestnuts, if desired. Turn mixture into a 1½-quart casserole.

Combine fine dry bread crumbs and 1 tablespoon melted margarine or butter; sprinkle atop casserole. Bake in 350° oven for 40 to 45 minutes or till heated through. Makes 4 to 6 servings.

Mackerel Fondue Bake

- 4 beaten eggs
- 2 cups *reconstituted* nonfat dry milk *or* milk
- ½ teaspoon prepared mustard
- 6 slices day-old bread, cut into ½-inch cubes (4 cups)
- 1 15½-ounce can mackerel *or* salmon, drained, broken up, bones and skin removed
- 1 cup shredded Swiss *or* American cheese *or* process cheese spread
- 1 8¾-ounce can whole kernel corn, drained
- ¼ cup finely chopped onion
- ¼ cup chopped celery
- Paprika (optional)

In large bowl combine eggs, milk, mustard, and 1 teaspoon *salt*. Stir in bread cubes, mackerel or salmon, shredded cheese, corn, onion, and celery. Turn into 8x8x2-inch baking dish or pan. Let stand 1 hour at room temperature or several hours in the refrigerator. Bake in 325° oven for 55 to 60 minutes or till knife inserted just off-center comes out clean. Let stand 5 minutes before serving. Sprinkle with paprika, if desired. Makes 6 to 8 servings.

Curried Tuna

- ½ of a 10-ounce package (1 cup) frozen peas *or* one 8½-ounce can peas
- ¼ cup chopped onion
- ¼ cup chopped celery
- ¼ cup margarine *or* butter
- ¼ cup all-purpose flour
- 1½ to 2 teaspoons curry powder
- 2 cups *reconstituted* nonfat dry milk *or* milk
- 1 9¼-ounce can tuna, drained and flaked
- Toast points

Cook frozen peas according to package directions; drain. (Or, drain canned peas.) Set aside.

In saucepan cook onion and celery in margarine or butter till vegetables are crisp-tender. Blend in flour, curry powder, and ¾ teaspoon *salt*. Add milk all at once. Cook and stir till thickened. Stir in tuna and drained peas. Heat through. Serve over toast points. Garnish with snipped parsley, if desired. Makes 6 servings.

Swiss-Tuna Burgers

- 1 beaten egg
- ¼ cup nonfat dry milk *powder*
- ¼ cup water
- 1 tablespoon catsup
- 1 tablespoon prepared mustard
- ½ teaspoon salt
- 1½ cups soft bread crumbs (2 slices)
- ¼ cup chopped celery
- 2 tablespoons finely chopped onion
- 1 9¼-ounce can tuna, drained and flaked
- 6 slices Swiss cheese
- 6 hamburger buns, split and toasted
- Salad dressing *or* mayonnaise (optional)

In bowl combine egg, nonfat dry milk powder, water, catsup, mustard, and salt. Stir in bread crumbs, celery, and onion. Add tuna; mix well. Shape into six patties, about 3 inches in diameter. Place on greased unheated broiler pan. Broil 5 inches from the heat for 6 to 7 minutes or till heated through. Top with cheese; broil 1 to 2 minutes more or till cheese begins to melt. Spread salad dressing or mayonnaise on hamburger buns, if desired. Place a tuna burger on bottom half of each bun; replace tops of buns. Makes 6 sandwiches.

Meatless Main Dishes

Buying Eggs

Eggs can play a versatile role in a meatless meal. Nutritionally, eggs are excellent sources of protein, calcium, and iron. One egg contains as much protein as 1 ounce of meat, poultry, or fish.

Eggs are sold in several sizes, from small to extra large and jumbo. Compare prices of different sizes, buying according to your needs.

To economize, never throw away even one extra egg yolk—leftover raw egg yolks can be used in cream puddings and fillings, custards, sauces, eggnog, homemade noodles, salad dressings, and scrambled eggs and omelets. In the above

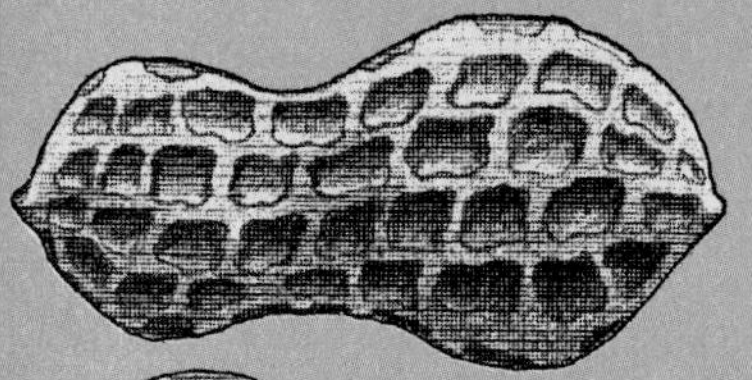

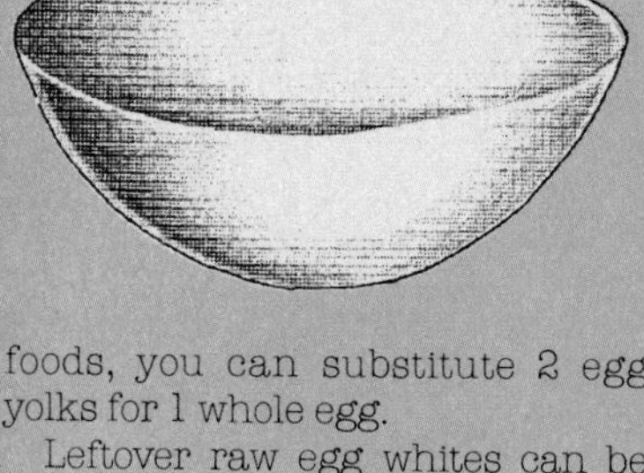

foods, you can substitute 2 egg yolks for 1 whole egg.

Leftover raw egg whites can be used in angel cakes, fluffy frostings, meringues, candies, glazes, and foamy sauces. Extra hard-cooked eggs, chopped or sliced, make delicious additions to cas-

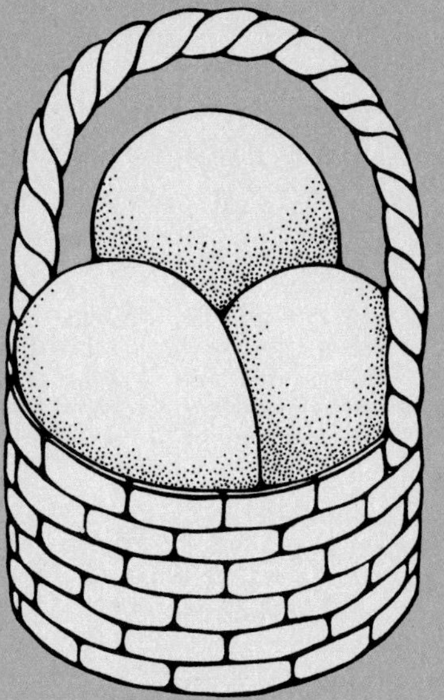

seroles, salads, and sandwiches. As a garnish, hard-cooked egg slices or wedges add a dash of color.

Choosing Cheese

Cheeses can be an economical way to boost the protein (and the calcium and riboflavin) in a meal.

Cheese is available in several types. To get the most from the money you spend, remember:

—Process cheese (a blend of fresh and aged natural cheeses) is often less expensive than natural cheese, especially if the natural cheese is labeled aged or sharp.

—Process cheese spread has more water and a lower percentage of cheese than process or natural cheese, and is usually less expensive.

—It's more expensive to buy any cheese that is already grated, shredded, or sliced.

Using Legumes

Try a main dish using dried beans, peas, lentils, or other legumes for an occasional alternative to eating meat, poultry, or fish. These vegetables are economical sources of protein, and provide tasty variety to your menu.

Add an animal food rich in high-quality protein such as eggs, cheese, or other dairy products to give the vegetable protein in a meal an extra boost. By including these in the meatless meal, complete protein is provided.

As an occasional alternative to using eggs or dairy products as your source of protein in the meal, the combination of dried beans, peas, or other legumes with whole grain or enriched breads and cereals will provide complete protein. Based on protein content, substitute 1/2 cup dried beans, peas, or other legumes for *1 ounce* meat.

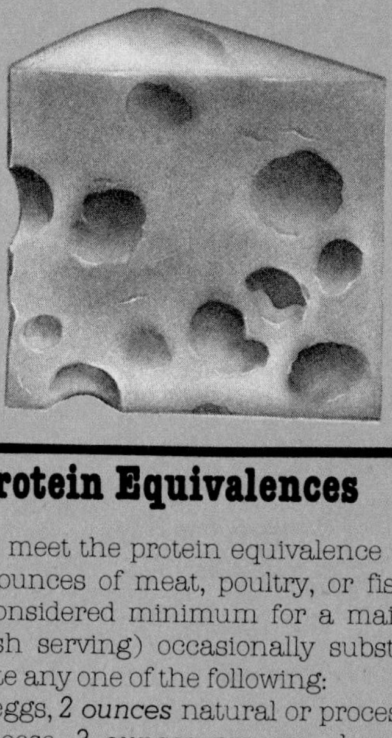

Protein Equivalences

To meet the protein equivalence of 2 ounces of meat, poultry, or fish (considered minimum for a main dish serving) occasionally substitute any one of the following: *2* eggs, *2 ounces* natural or process cheese, *3 ounces* process cheese spread, *1/2 cup* cottage cheese, *1 1/2 cups* milk, *1/4 cup* peanut butter, or *1 cup* cooked legumes.

For variety, choose a combination of the above meatless alternatives. Just be sure you get the protein equivalence of 2 ounces of meat. We've included recipes in this chapter calculated to give you 2 ounces protein per main-dish serving.

Main Dish Pasta Ring

Pictured on pages 10 and 11—

- Shortening
- 1/3 cup fine dry bread crumbs
- 8 ounces medium noodles
- 1 cup shredded carrot
- 1/2 cup chopped onion
- 3 tablespoons margarine *or* butter
- 3 tablespoons all-purpose flour
- 3/4 teaspoon salt
- 1/2 teaspoon ground sage *or* dried dillweed
- 1/8 teaspoon pepper
- 1 1/2 cups *reconstituted* nonfat dry milk *or* milk
- 1 cup shredded American cheese *or* process cheese spread (4 ounces)
- 1 4-ounce can mushroom stems and pieces, drained and chopped
- 2 beaten eggs
- Tomato-Cheese Sauce (see recipe at right)
- Snipped parsley (optional)

Generously grease a 6 1/2-cup ring mold with shortening; sprinkle with bread crumbs till well-coated. (Or, generously grease six 1 1/2-cup molds or 10-ounce custard cups; sprinkle with crumbs till well-coated.) Set aside.

Cook noodles in boiling salted water according to package directions; drain well. Set aside.

In large saucepan cook carrot and onion in margarine or butter till onion is tender. Blend in flour, salt, sage or dillweed, and pepper. Add the milk all at once; cook and stir till thickened and bubbly. Cook and stir 1 minute more. Add cheese and mushrooms, stirring till cheese is melted.

Stir about *half* of the hot sauce mixture into beaten eggs; return all to saucepan. Fold in cooked noodles. Spoon mixture into prepared ring mold or individual molds; place in a larger pan. Pour hot water into pan around mold(s) to depth of 1 inch. Cover; bake in 350° oven for 35 to 40 minutes or till knife inserted near center comes out clean. Remove pan from oven; remove mold(s) from water. Let stand 5 minutes. Loosen noodle mixture from the outside and center of ring mold by running a narrow metal spatula around the edges. Invert onto serving platter. Cut mold into 6 portions. (Or, invert individual molds onto serving plates.) Serve with Tomato-Cheese Sauce spooned over. Garnish with parsley, if desired. Makes 6 servings.

Tomato-Cheese Sauce

This sauce is equally delicious spooned over beef patties, too—

- 2 tablespoons margarine *or* butter
- 2 tablespoons all-purpose flour
- 1/4 teaspoon salt
- Dash pepper
- 1 cup *reconstituted* nonfat dry milk *or* milk
- 1 cup shredded American cheese *or* process cheese spread (4 ounces)
- 1 large tomato, peeled, seeded, and chopped

In small heavy saucepan melt margarine or butter. Blend in flour, salt, and pepper. Add milk all at once. Cook and stir over medium heat till thickened and bubbly. Cook and stir 2 minutes more. Remove from heat; stir in shredded American cheese or process cheese spread till melted. Stir in chopped tomato; heat through. Makes about 2 1/3 cups sauce.

Cheesy Broccoli Bake

This zesty casserole is rich in protein from dairy foods—

- 6 ounces medium noodles
- 1 10-ounce package frozen chopped broccoli *or* spinach
- 1 1/2 cups cream-style cottage cheese (12 ounces)
- 1 cup dairy sour cream (8 ounces)
- 1/2 cup grated parmesan cheese
- 1 beaten egg
- 1/4 cup *reconstituted* nonfat dry milk *or* milk
- 1 teaspoon salt
- 1/2 teaspoon dried basil, crushed
- 1/2 teaspoon dried thyme, crushed
- 1/4 to 1/2 teaspoon bottled hot pepper sauce
- 1/4 cup fine dry bread crumbs
- 1 tablespoon margarine *or* butter, melted
- Snipped parsley (optional)

Cook noodles according to package directions; drain well. In saucepan cook chopped broccoli or spinach in boiling salted water about 4 minutes or till broccoli or spinach has *just separated*; drain well, pressing out extra liquid.

In large mixing bowl stir together broccoli or spinach, cottage cheese, sour cream, parmesan cheese, beaten egg, milk, salt, basil, thyme, and hot pepper sauce. Add cooked and drained noodles; mix well. Turn noodle-cheese mixture into ungreased 2-quart casserole.

Toss together dry bread crumbs and melted margarine or butter. Sprinkle atop casserole. Bake in 350° oven about 45 minutes or till heated through. Garnish with parsley, if desired. Makes 6 servings.

Meatless Italian Lasagne

¼ cup margarine *or* butter
2 medium carrots, finely chopped
2 stalks celery, finely chopped
1 medium green pepper, chopped
2 medium onions, chopped
2 medium zucchini, sliced
1 16-ounce can tomatoes, cut up
1 12-ounce can tomato paste
2 bay leaves
2 *or* 3 cloves garlic, minced
¼ cup snipped parsley
1 teaspoon dried basil, crushed
¾ teaspoon salt
½ teaspoon dried oregano, crushed
½ teaspoon dried thyme, crushed
¼ teaspoon pepper
2 cups sliced fresh mushrooms (optional)
10 lasagne noodles, cooked, rinsed, and drained (about 8 ounces)
2 cups cream-style cottage cheese, drained
8 slices mozzarella cheese, torn (8 ounces)
¼ cup grated parmesan cheese

In large saucepan melt margarine or butter. Stir in carrots, celery, green pepper, and onion. Cover and cook for 10 minutes, stirring frequently. Add zucchini, *undrained* tomatoes, and tomato paste; mix well. Add bay leaves, garlic, parsley, and seasonings. Cover and simmer for 30 minutes; remove cover and continue simmering 10 to 15 minutes more or till thickened to desired consistency. Stir in sliced mushrooms, if desired; cook 5 minutes more. Remove from heat; discard bay leaves.

In 13x9x2-inch baking pan layer *one-third* of the noodles, vegetable sauce, cottage cheese, and mozzarella. Repeat twice, ending with mozzarella on top. Sprinkle parmesan over all. Cover with foil; place on baking sheet.

Bake in 350° oven 45 minutes; remove foil and continue baking 10 minutes more or till cheese is golden. Remove from oven; let stand 10 minutes before serving. If desired, garnish with snipped parsley. Makes 8 to 10 servings.

◀ Brimming with vegetables, *Meatless Italian Lasagne* is delightfully seasoned with herbs and spices.

Choose-a-Filling Omelet

1 tablespoon margarine
1 tablespoon all-purpose flour
⅔ cup *reconstituted* nonfat dry milk *or* milk
¼ cup shredded American *or* Swiss cheese *or* 2 tablespoons grated parmesan cheese
6 eggs
4 teaspoons margarine
Desired omelet filling (see below)

For cheese sauce, in saucepan melt 1 tablespoon margarine. Blend in flour, ⅛ teaspoon *salt*, and ⅛ teaspoon *pepper*. Add milk all at once. Cook and stir till thickened and bubbly. Stir in cheese; heat till cheese melts. Cover and keep warm while preparing omelets.

To make omelets, beat together eggs, 2 tablespoons *water*, ½ teaspoon *salt*, and ⅛ teaspoon *pepper* with a fork till mixture is blended but not frothy.

In 10-inch skillet melt *2 teaspoons* of the margarine; heat till margarine sizzles and browns slightly; tilt pan to grease sides. Add *half* the egg mixture. Cook over medium heat. As eggs set, run a spatula around edge and lift eggs to allow uncooked portion to flow underneath. When eggs are set but still shiny, remove from heat. Spoon desired omelet filling across center; fold both sides over filling. Tilt pan to roll omelet out onto plate; keep warm. Repeat to make second omelet. Spoon *half* of cheese sauce over each. Makes 4 servings.

Cottage Omelet: Combine 1 cup *dry curd cottage cheese*, ⅓ cup finely shredded *carrot*, 2 tablespoons chopped *onion*, and 2 tablespoons *salad dressing or mayonnaise*. Fill each omelet with *half* the cottage cheese mixture.

Spinach Omelet: Before preparing cheese sauce and omelets, cook ½ of a 10-ounce package frozen *chopped spinach* according to package directions. Drain well. Combine spinach, 3 tablespoons *dairy sour cream*, ¼ teaspoon *salt*, and dash ground *nutmeg*. Keep mixture warm while preparing sauce and omelets. Fill each omelet with *half* spinach mixture.

Garden Omelet: Combine 1 cup *cooked vegetable* (use your choice) with ½ teaspoon dried *thyme*, crushed. Prepare cheese sauce; stir *¼ cup* sauce into the vegetables. Heat through; keep mixture warm while preparing omelets. Fill each omelet with *half* of the vegetable mixture. Spoon remaining sauce atop omelets.

Summer Vegetable Omelet: Before preparing cheese sauce and omelets, in skillet cook ½ cup thinly sliced *zucchini*, ¼ cup chopped *green pepper*, and 2 tablespoons chopped *onion* in 2 tablespoons *margarine* till tender. Stir in 1 small *tomato*, peeled, seeded, and chopped, and ¼ teaspoon *salt*. Prepare cheese sauce; stir *¼ cup* sauce into cooked vegetables; keep mixture warm while preparing omelets. Fill each omelet with half the vegetable mixture. Spoon remaining sauce atop omelets.

Side Dishes & Desserts

This taste-tempting extravaganza of side dishes and desserts is (clockwise from back left) *Oven Calico Rice, Individual Chocolate Pies, Whole Wheat and Bran Rolls, Lemon and Cream Cheese Broccoli,* and *Salad Ambrosia.* (See index for recipe pages.)

Salads

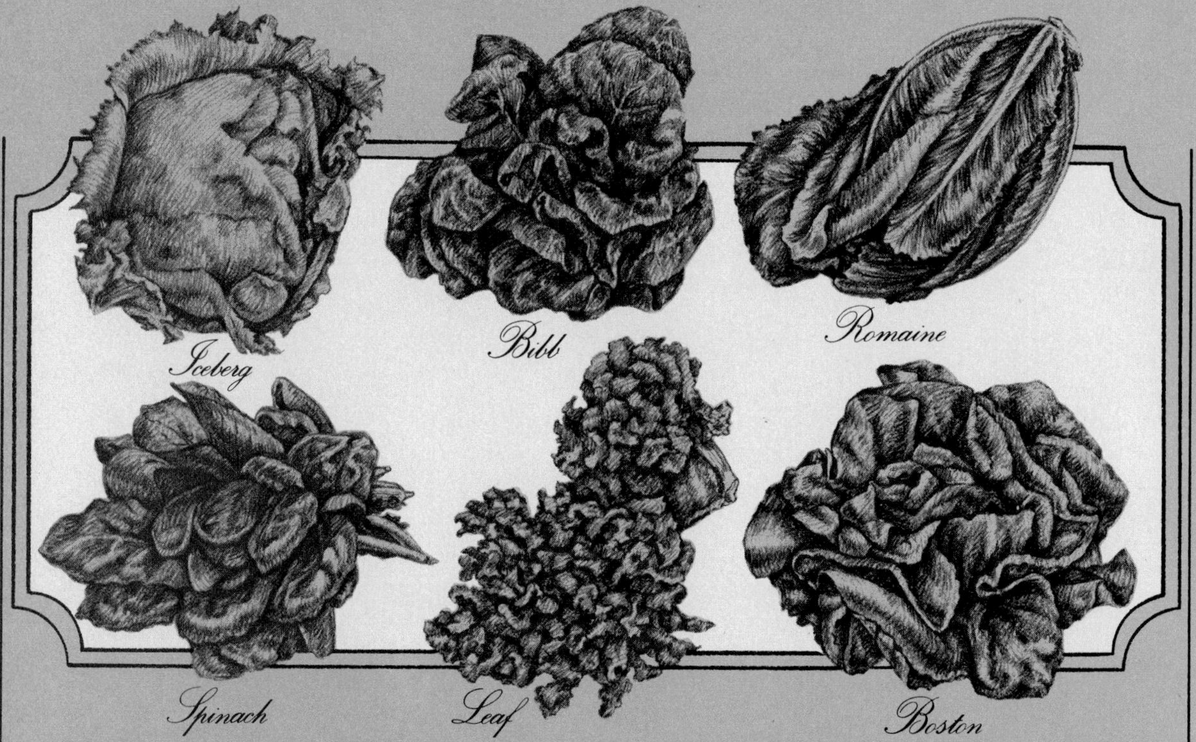

Need some meal-mates for the main dish? Start with a tempting salad. Try a fruit, vegetable, or gelatin salad combination to complement the main dish. Low cost needn't mean low quality, either. Buy fresh fruits and vegetables at their seasonal peak for lowest cost and highest quality. Check the chart on page 96 for the seasonal availability of a variety of fresh fruits and vegetables.

Don't Throw It Out!

Choose from the wide array of canned and frozen fruits and vegetables available all year round. For real economy, save the syrup drained off canned or thawed frozen fruits. Use it to make delicious dressings for fruit salads by combining it with salad dressing, mayonnaise, sour cream, or plain

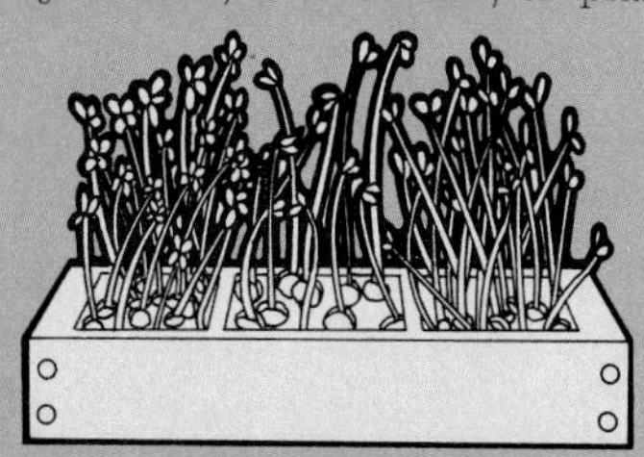

yogurt. Or, replace part of the water with the syrup when making gelatin salads.

Don't throw away small amounts of fruits—fresh, frozen, or canned. Use them as appetizing additions to gelatin salads, fruit cups, parfaits, or compotes. Or, try adding leftover cooked or raw vegetables to your favorite tossed salad for a new taste appeal. You'll be surprised at the infinite variety an assortment of fruits or vegetables can give to a simple, basic salad.

Don't limit your salad choices. Let your imagination as well as your common sense be the guide in planning nutritious and budget-minded salads for your family.

Salad Greens

Different salad greens may be economical at different seasons so compare prices when shopping.

To store salad greens, remove and discard wilted outer leaves. Separate leaf lettuce or remove the core from head lettuce for thorough rinsing. Rinse in cold water; drain. Place in a clean kitchen towel or paper toweling and pat dry. Place in plastic bag; refrigerate at least 8 hours to crisp the leaves. Before serving, tear greens into bite-size pieces; this allows the dressing to be absorbed by the greens. Place in salad bowl. To hold salad greens for a short time, cover with a damp paper towel and refrigerate till serving time.

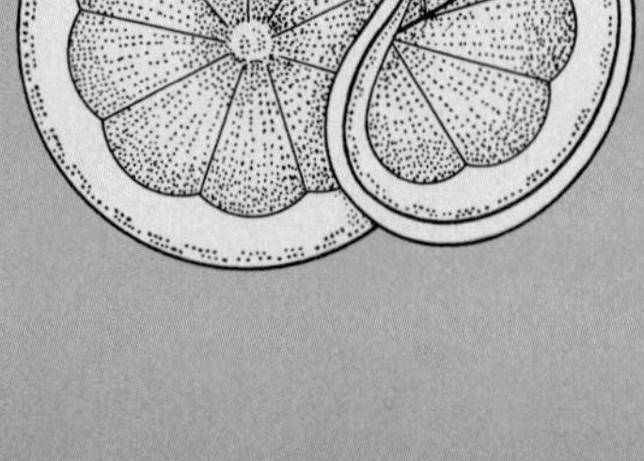

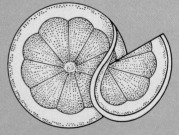

Mixed Vegetable Medley Salad

This tangy vegetable salad is a good make-ahead for busy days—

- 1 slice bread, cut into ½-inch cubes
- 2 tablespoons margarine *or* butter
- 1 10-ounce package frozen mixed vegetables *or* one 16-ounce can mixed vegetables
- ¼ cup vinegar
- 2 to 3 tablespoons sugar
- 1 tablespoon salad oil
- ¼ teaspoon salt
- ¼ teaspoon dry mustard
- ¼ teaspoon celery seed
- ⅛ teaspoon dried thyme, crushed
- Dash pepper
- 2 cups torn lettuce *or* assorted salad greens
- ½ small onion, sliced and separated into rings

In small skillet cook bread cubes in margarine or butter till golden brown and crisp; turn occasionally. Cool. Store in covered container in refrigerator.

Cook frozen mixed vegetables according to package directions; drain. (Or, drain canned mixed vegetables.) For marinade, in screw-top jar combine vinegar, sugar, salad oil, salt, dry mustard, celery seed, thyme, and pepper. Cover and shake to mix well. Pour marinade over mixed vegetables; stir gently to coat. Cover and refrigerate several hours or overnight.

At serving time, divide lettuce or salad greens among 4 individual serving bowls. Top each with ¼ of the *undrained* marinated mixed vegetables. Garnish each salad with some of the onion rings and toasted bread cubes. Makes 4 servings.

24-Hour Cabbage Salad

- 3 cups shredded cabbage
- ¼ cup chopped green pepper
- ¼ cup chopped onion
- ¼ cup shredded carrot
- ½ cup sugar
- ½ cup vinegar
- ¾ teaspoon mustard seed
- ¾ teaspoon celery seed
- ½ teaspoon salt
- Carrot curls

In mixing bowl combine cabbage, green pepper, onion, and carrot. Stir together sugar, vinegar, mustard seed, celery seed, and salt till sugar dissolves. Pour over cabbage mixture; toss well. Cover and chill at least 24 hours. Drain off dressing before serving. Garnish with carrot curls, if desired. Makes 6 servings.

Confetti Cottage Cheese-Tomato Salad

- 1½ cups cream-style cottage cheese (12 ounces)
- ¼ cup finely chopped green pepper
- ¼ cup finely shredded carrot
- 2 tablespoons finely chopped onion
- ¼ teaspoon salt
- ¼ cup salad dressing *or* mayonnaise
- Lettuce
- Tomato wedges *or* cherry tomatoes, halved

In bowl combine cottage cheese, green pepper, carrot, onion, and salt. Stir in salad dressing or mayonnaise; cover and chill. Serve cottage cheese mixture on individual lettuce-lined plates. Garnish with tomato wedges or cherry tomatoes. Makes 4 servings.

Potato Salad-Stuffed Tomatoes

This tempting salad is a combination of two summer favorites—

- 3 medium potatoes
- 3 slices bacon
- 1 hard-cooked egg, chopped
- ¼ cup chopped celery
- 3 tablespoons finely chopped onion
- ½ cup salad dressing *or* mayonnaise
- 2 teaspoons vinegar
- ¼ teaspoon salt
- Dash pepper
- 6 medium tomatoes
- Lettuce
- Hard-cooked egg slices (optional)
- Parsley sprigs (optional)

In covered saucepan cook potatoes in boiling salted water for 25 to 40 minutes or till tender; drain. Set aside to cool before peeling. Meanwhile, in small skillet cook bacon slices till crisp. Drain, crumble, and set aside.

Peel and cube potatoes. Combine potatoes, chopped hard-cooked egg, celery, onion, and crumbled bacon. Combine salad dressing or mayonnaise, vinegar, salt, and pepper; toss with potato mixture. Cover and chill.

To prepare tomato cups, place tomatoes, stem side down, on cutting surface. With sharp knife, cut tomato into 4 to 6 wedges, cutting to, but not through, the base of tomato. Spread tomato wedges apart slightly; sprinkle with a little salt. Cover and chill tomatoes.

To serve, place chilled tomatoes on individual lettuce-lined plates. Fill each tomato cup with *about ½ cup* of the potato salad mixture. Garnish each salad with a few hard-cooked egg slices and a parsley sprig, if desired. Makes 6 servings.

Patchword Potato Salad

4 medium potatoes
1 10-ounce package frozen chopped broccoli
3 carrots, chopped (about 1 cup)
½ cup salad dressing *or* mayonnaise
¼ cup chopped onion
½ teaspoon salt
1 hard-cooked egg, sliced

Cook potatoes in boiling salted water about 30 minutes or till tender. Drain; cool slightly. Peel and cube potatoes. Season with a little salt and pepper to taste; set aside. In covered saucepan cook broccoli and carrots in *½ cup* boiling salted water for 10 to 15 minutes or till crisp-tender, *do not drain*. Add salad dressing or mayonnaise, onion, and the ½ teaspoon salt to broccoli and carrots; mix well. Toss broccoli mixture with potatoes. Chill. Garnish with egg slices to serve. Makes 4 servings.

Chili Mac Salad

1 cup elbow macaroni
1 15 ½-ounce can red kidney beans, drained
¾ cup chopped celery
½ cup shredded carrot
2 tablespoons finely chopped onion
⅔ cup salad dressing *or* mayonnaise
2 tablespoons *reconstituted* nonfat dry milk *or* milk
1½ teaspoons chili powder
½ teaspoon salt
½ teaspoon dried oregano, crushed
Dash garlic powder
Few drops bottled hot pepper sauce
Lettuce (optional)

Cook macaroni in boiling salted water according to package directions; drain. Rinse with cold water to cool macaroni; drain again. Combine macaroni, kidney beans, celery, carrot, and onion. Blend together salad dressing or mayonnaise, milk, chili powder, salt, oregano, garlic powder, and bottled hot pepper sauce. Add to macaroni mixture; stir gently to blend. Cover; chill several hours. To serve, spoon into lettuce-lined bowl, if desired. Makes 6 to 8 servings.

Mostaccioli Salad

8 ounces mostaccioli *or* 2½ cups elbow *or* shell macaroni
2 small onions, thinly sliced and separated into rings
1 small cucumber, thinly sliced
⅔ cup vinegar
½ cup sugar
3 tablespoons salad oil
1 tablespoon snipped parsley
½ teaspoon salt
½ teaspoon dry mustard
⅛ teaspoon garlic powder
Dash pepper
1 small tomato

Cook mostaccioli or other pasta according to package directions; drain. Rinse with cold water to cool pasta; drain again. In bowl combine cooked mostaccioli or other pasta, sliced onion, and sliced cucumber. In screw-top jar combine vinegar, sugar, salad oil, parsley, salt, mustard, garlic powder, and pepper; cover and shake to mix well. Pour vinegar mixture over pasta and vegetables; stir lightly. Cover and refrigerate several hours or overnight, stirring occasionally. Peel tomato; seed and chop. To serve, drain pasta and vegetable mixture; stir in tomato. Makes 6 to 8 servings.

Corn Salad

1 17-ounce can whole kernel corn, drained
2 ounces cheddar *or* Swiss cheese *or* process cheese spread, cut into ¼-inch cubes (½ cup)
¼ cup chopped green pepper
¼ cup chopped onion
¼ cup chopped cucumber
¼ cup sweet pickle relish
½ cup thousand island salad dressing
Lettuce

In a bowl combine drained corn, cheese cubes, green pepper, onion, cucumber, and pickle relish. Fold in dressing. Cover; chill several hours or overnight. Serve in lettuce cups. Makes 5 or 6 servings.

Citrus Yogurt Squares

1 16-ounce can pear slices *or* halves
1 6-ounce package *or* two 3-ounce packages lime-flavored gelatin
1 medium banana, sliced
1 cup lemon yogurt
Lettuce

Drain pears, reserving syrup. Add cold water to syrup, if necessary, to make ¾ cup liquid. Dissolve gelatin in 2 cups *boiling water*. Set aside *1 cup* gelatin mixture; keep at room temperature. Stir reserved syrup into remaining gelatin; chill till partially set. Chop pears; fold pears and banana into partially set gelatin. Pour into 8x8x2-inch or 9x9x2-inch pan. Chill till almost firm. Beat reserved gelatin mixture into yogurt. Spoon over pear layer in pan. Chill till firm. Cut into squares and serve on lettuce-lined plates. Serves 9 to 12.

Salad Ambrosia

This cool and refreshing salad is pictured on pages 60 and 61—

- 1 6-ounce package *or* two 3-ounce packages apricot-flavored gelatin
- 2 cups boiling water
- 1 12-ounce can (1½ cups) lemon-lime carbonated beverage
- 1 10-ounce package frozen sliced strawberries, partially thawed
- 1 8¼-ounce can crushed pineapple
- 2 bananas, sliced
- Whipped topping (optional)

Dissolve apricot gelatin in the boiling water. Gently stir in carbonated beverage. Chill till partially set (consistency of unbeaten egg whites). Fold in *undrained* strawberries, *undrained* pineapple, and sliced bananas. Turn gelatin mixture into a 6½-cup mold or twelve individual ½-cup molds. Chill several hours or overnight till firm. Garnish with whipped topping, if desired. Makes 12 servings.

Fruit Medley with Pineapple Dressing

- 1 15½-ounce can pineapple chunks
- 2 tablespoons sugar
- 1 tablespoon cornstarch
- Dash salt
- 1 teaspoon lemon juice
- ¼ cup salad dressing *or* mayonnaise
- 1 16-ounce can peach slices, chilled
- 1 16-ounce can pear slices, chilled
- 1 16-ounce can jellied cranberry sauce, chilled
- Lettuce

To make dressing, drain pineapple chunks, reserving liquid; chill pineapple. Add water to liquid, if necessary, to make ¾ cup.

In saucepan combine sugar, cornstarch, and salt. Stir in reserved pineapple liquid. Cook, stirring constantly, till mixture is thickened and bubbly; cook 1 minute more. Remove saucepan from heat; stir in lemon juice. Cool. Blend in salad dressing or mayonnaise. Cover dressing and chill.

To serve, drain peaches and pears; cut cranberry sauce into 1-inch cubes. Arrange pineapple chunks, peach slices, pear slices, and cranberry sauce cubes on individual lettuce-lined plates. Pass chilled pineapple dressing. Makes 8 servings.

Crunch-Top Fruit Salad

The toasted oat topping has a nutlike flavor, and goes well on ice cream, too—

- 1 tablespoon margarine *or* butter
- ⅓ cup rolled oats
- 2 tablespoons brown sugar
- ⅛ teaspoon ground cinnamon
- Dash ground nutmeg
- 3 oranges
- 3 apples
- 2 bananas
- ½ cup chopped celery
- Lettuce
- ½ cup dairy sour cream
- 1½ teaspoons granulated sugar

For oat topping, in 8x8x2-inch baking pan melt margarine or butter; stir in rolled oats, brown sugar, cinnamon, and nutmeg; mix well. Bake in 350° oven about 20 minutes or till lightly browned, stirring occasionally. Cool in pan.

Peel, section, and cut up oranges over a bowl, reserving juice. Core and chop apples; peel and slice bananas. Dip apples and bananas in reserved orange juice to coat. Combine oranges, apples, bananas, and celery.

For dressing, stir together sour cream and granulated sugar; fold into fruit mixture. Turn into a lettuce-lined salad bowl. Sprinkle with cooled oat topping just before serving. Makes 8 to 10 servings.

Fruit Cocktail Freeze

- 1 cup orange, strawberry, *or* peach yogurt
- 3 tablespoons sugar
- 1 8¾-ounce can fruit cocktail, drained
- ¼ cup finely chopped celery
- Lettuce

In mixing bowl stir together yogurt and sugar. Fold in fruit cocktail and celery. Spoon mixture into 4 individual molds or paper bake cup-lined muffin pans. Cover and freeze till firm. To serve, let stand at room temperature for 10 minutes. Unmold or peel off paper. Serve on lettuce-lined salad plates. Makes 4 servings.

Cucumber Salad

This salad is of Lebanese origin—

- 1 cup plain yogurt
- 2 tablespoons salad oil
- 4 teaspoons lemon juice
- 4 teaspoons dried mint, crushed *or* 2 tablespoons snipped fresh mint
- 2 cups thinly sliced cucumber
- Lettuce (optional)

Stir together yogurt, salad oil, lemon juice, and mint. Add to sliced cucumber; toss to combine. Cover and chill. Serve cucumber mixture in lettuce-lined salad bowl, if desired. Makes 4 servings.

Vegetables

Delicious budget vegetable fix-ups are easy with the endless variety offered by fresh, frozen, and canned vegetables. Compare cost per serving for the best buy when choosing among these varieties.

Buying Fresh Vegetables

Buy fresh vegetables during the season when abundance is greatest and price is lowest. (See the chart on page 96.) But limit your fresh produce purchases to amounts you will use within a few days.

Buying Potatoes

Potatoes are available all year at a reasonable cost. Compare the price of all-purpose versus baking potatoes. Usually, all-purpose potatoes are lower priced and can be used in all types of dishes.

Storing Vegetables

Store potatoes, onions, and winter squash in a cool, dry place. Store all other fresh vegetables in your refrigerator.

Frozen Vegetables

Save on frozen vegetables by comparing prices. Large bags of frozen vegetables usually cost less per ounce. And, you can simply pour out the amount you need and return the rest to the freezer.

For the best quality frozen vegetables, select packages stored below the designated load line in the store's freezer case. Or choose vegetables stored toward the back of the freezer. Watch for frost on vegetable packages or inside a plastic bag of vegetables; this indicates thawing (and loss of nutrients) may have occurred. At home, keep the vegetables frozen until you're ready to use them.

Canned Vegetables

Oftentimes canned vegetables are your best buy. Select canned vegetables that are best suited for your purpose; some cut or chopped vegetables cost less than whole vegetables because they don't require an entire vegetable to be perfect. And, there's no difference in flavor or nutrition between vegetable pieces and whole vegetables.

Here are a few easy ideas for dressing up everyday vegetables:

—Cook vegetables in beef or chicken broth instead of water.

—Sprinkle vegetables with buttered bread crumbs or croutons.

—Top vegetables with a cheese sauce or sprinkle them with a little shredded cheese.

—For extra crunch, add chopped celery, green pepper, or green onion to cooked vegetables.

Save the cooking liquid from vegetables or the liquid drained off canned vegetables. Some nutrients, especially vitamin C and some minerals, are present in this liquid. It can be frozen for a delicious and nutritious addition to stocks, soups, gravies, and sauces.

Spinach-Green Bean Casserole

- 1 10-ounce package frozen chopped spinach, thawed
- 1 9-ounce package frozen cut green beans, thawed *or* one 16-ounce can green beans
- 1 medium onion, chopped
- 1/4 cup water
- 1 clove garlic, minced
- 1 teaspoon salt
- 1 teaspoon dried basil, crushed
- 1/8 teaspoon ground nutmeg
- 1/8 teaspoon pepper
- 3 beaten eggs
- 1/4 cup grated parmesan cheese
- Paprika

Drain spinach and green beans well. In large skillet combine spinach, beans, onion, water, garlic, salt, basil, nutmeg, and pepper. Cover; simmer for 10 minutes, stirring occasionally. Remove from heat. Gradually stir vegetable mixture into the beaten eggs; mix well. Turn into an 8x1 1/2-inch round baking dish. Bake, uncovered, in 350° oven about 15 minutes or till set. Sprinkle with parmesan and paprika. Bake for 2 to 3 minutes more. Makes 6 servings.

Stuffed Baked Potatoes

- 4 medium potatoes (about 1 1/4 pounds)
- 1/4 cup chopped onion
- 2 tablespoons margarine *or* butter, melted
- *Reconstituted* nonfat dry milk *or* milk
- 1/2 cup shredded American *or* Swiss cheese *or* process cheese spread (2 ounces)
- 2 tablespoons snipped parsley
- Paprika

Scrub potatoes thoroughly and prick with a fork. Bake in 425° oven for 40 to 60 minutes or till potatoes are tender.

Cut a lengthwise slice from top of each potato; discard skin from slice. Reserving potato shells, scoop out the insides, leaving a 1/4 inch shell. Add to potato portions from top slices; mash.

Cook onion in margarine or butter till tender; add to mashed potatoes. Beat in enough milk to make a fluffy consistency. Season potatoes to taste with salt and pepper; stir in cheese and parsley.

Pile mashed potato mixture into potato shells. Place in 10x6x2-inch baking dish. Bake in 425° oven for 20 to 25 minutes or till lightly browned. Sprinkle with paprika. Makes 4 servings.

Lemon and Cream Cheese Broccoli

This elegant vegetable is pictured on pages 60 and 61. Try the sauce with brussels sprouts or green beans, too—

- 2 tablespoons margarine *or* butter
- 1 tablespoon all-purpose flour
- 1/4 teaspoon salt
- 1/8 teaspoon ground ginger
- Dash ground nutmeg
- 1 1/4 cups *reconstituted* nonfat dry milk *or* milk
- 1 3-ounce package cream cheese, cut up
- 1/2 teaspoon finely shredded lemon peel (optional)
- 1 tablespoon lemon juice
- 3 10-ounce packages frozen broccoli spears *or* 2 1/4 pounds fresh broccoli
- Shredded lemon peel (optional)

In saucepan melt margarine or butter. Blend in flour, salt, ginger, and nutmeg. Add milk all at once. Cook and stir till thickened and bubbly. Reduce heat; blend in cream cheese till smooth. Stir in the 1/2 teaspoon lemon peel and the lemon juice. Keep sauce warm while preparing broccoli.

Cook frozen broccoli according to package directions. (Or, cut fresh broccoli into spears. In covered saucepan cook broccoli in small amount of boiling salted water for 10 to 15 minutes or till crisp-tender.) Drain well. Arrange broccoli on serving platter. Drizzle with some of the sauce; sprinkle with additional lemon peel, if desired. Pass remaining sauce. Makes 8 to 10 servings.

Carrot-Rutabaga Bake

Serve this rich-tasting dish the next time you have company—

- 1 large rutabaga, peeled and cubed
- 3 large carrots, shredded
- 1 egg
- 2 tablespoons margarine *or* butter
- 1 tablespoon brown sugar
- 1 teaspoon salt
- Dash pepper
- 1 cup evaporated milk
- 1 cup cooked rice

In covered saucepan cook rutabaga in boiling salted water for 25 to 30 minutes or till tender; drain. Meanwhile, cook shredded carrots in boiling salted water about 5 minutes or till almost tender. Drain and set aside.

With electric mixer whip rutabaga, egg, margarine or butter, brown sugar, salt, and pepper till fluffy. Stir in milk; fold in rice and carrots. Turn into 10x6x2-inch baking dish. Bake, uncovered, in 350° oven for 35 to 40 minutes or till heated through. Makes 12 servings.

Cheese Scalloped Corn

Cheese and eggs add richness to this corn casserole—

1 10-ounce package frozen whole kernel corn *or* one 17-ounce can whole kernel corn, drained
1/4 cup chopped onion
1/4 cup chopped green pepper
2 tablespoons margarine *or* butter
2 tablespoons all-purpose flour
1/2 teaspoon salt
1/4 teaspoon dry mustard
Dash pepper
3/4 cup *reconstituted* nonfat dry milk *or* milk
1 cup shredded American *or* cheddar cheese *or* process cheese spread (4 ounces)
2 beaten eggs
1/4 cup fine dry bread crumbs
1 tablespoon margarine *or* butter, melted

Cook frozen corn according to package directions; drain well. (Or, drain canned corn.)

For cheese sauce, in saucepan cook onion and green pepper in the 2 tablespoons margarine or butter till onion is tender but not brown. Blend in flour, salt, dry mustard, and pepper. Add milk all at once; cook and stir till thickened and bubbly. Add cheese, stirring till melted.

Combine corn and beaten eggs; stir into cheese sauce. Turn mixture into a 1-quart casserole. Combine bread crumbs and the 1 tablespoon melted margarine or butter; sprinkle over casserole. Bake in 350° oven about 45 minutes or till bubbly. Let stand for 5 to 10 minutes before serving. Makes 6 servings.

Broccoli-Potato Bake

2 tablespoons margarine
2 tablespoons all-purpose flour
1 teaspoon salt
1/8 teaspoon pepper
1/8 teaspoon ground nutmeg
2 cups *reconstituted* nonfat dry milk *or* milk
1 3-ounce package cream cheese, cut up
1/2 cup shredded Swiss *or* American cheese *or* process cheese spread
3 cups cubed cooked potatoes
1 10-ounce package frozen chopped broccoli, cooked and drained
1/4 cup fine dry bread crumbs
1 tablespoon margarine, melted

Melt the 2 tablespoons margarine; blend in flour, salt, pepper, and nutmeg. Add milk all at once; cook and stir till thickened and bubbly. Add cheeses, stirring till melted. Stir in potatoes. Turn *half* of the mixture into 10x6x2-inch baking dish; top with broccoli. Spoon remaining potato mixture over. Cover; bake in 350° oven 35 minutes. Mix crumbs and the 1 tablespoon melted margarine; sprinkle atop. Bake, uncovered, 10 to 15 minutes more. Makes 8 servings.

Baked Beans and Apple

1 medium apple, peeled, cored, and sliced (3/4 cup)
1/2 cup chopped onion
1 16-ounce can pork and beans in tomato sauce
2 tablespoons raisins (optional)
1 tablespoon catsup
1 teaspoon prepared mustard
1/8 teaspoon ground cinnamon

In small saucepan cook apple slices and onion in small amount of boiling water about 5 minutes or till apple is crisp-tender; drain. In mixing bowl combine cooked apple and onion, pork and beans, raisins, catsup, prepared mustard, and cinnamon. Turn bean mixture into a 1-quart casserole or bean pot. Bake, uncovered, in 350° oven about 45 minutes or till heated through, stirring once. Makes 4 servings.

Deluxe Creamed Peas with Onion

2 medium onions, cut into wedges
1 10-ounce package frozen peas *or* one 16-ounce can peas, drained
1/2 cup shredded carrot
1 tablespoon margarine *or* butter
1 tablespoon all-purpose flour
1/2 teaspoon salt
1/8 teaspoon pepper
1 cup *reconstituted* nonfat dry milk *or* milk

Cook onions in boiling salted water for 10 minutes. Add frozen peas; cook for 5 to 10 minutes more or till vegetables are tender. (If using canned peas, cook onions for 15 to 20 minutes or till tender. Add peas; heat through.) Drain well; keep warm.

Meanwhile, in another saucepan cook carrot in margarine or butter about 5 minutes or till tender. Blend in flour, salt, and pepper. Add milk all at once; cook and stir till thickened and bubbly. Cook 1 minute more. Stir in drained onions and peas; heat through. Makes 6 servings.

Ratatouille-Style Vegetables

Similar to classic ratatouille, but without expensive eggplant—

1 medium onion, cut into thin wedges
1 clove garlic, minced
1 tablespoon cooking oil
1 7½-ounce can tomatoes, cut up
1 medium potato, peeled, halved lengthwise, and sliced
¾ teaspoon dried thyme, crushed
½ teaspoon salt
⅛ teaspoon pepper
1 medium zucchini, cut into bite-size strips (2 cups)
1 medium green pepper, cut into thin strips (1 cup)

In 2-quart saucepan cook onion wedges and garlic in oil till tender. Add the *undrained* tomatoes, sliced potato, thyme, salt, and pepper. Cover and simmer for 15 minutes; add the zucchini and green pepper strips. Cover and cook for 15 minutes more or till vegetables are tender. Serve hot or cold. Makes 4 servings.

Winter Carrot Casserole

Horseradish and mayonnaise add character to baked carrots—

1½ pounds carrots, sliced (4½ cups)
½ cup salad dressing *or* mayonnaise
2 tablespoons chopped onion
2 tablespoons prepared horseradish
¼ teaspoon salt
Dash pepper
¼ cup crushed saltine crackers (7 crackers)
2 teaspoons margarine *or* butter, melted

In covered saucepan cook carrots in boiling salted water about 10 minutes or till tender; drain. Place in 1-quart casserole.

Combine salad dressing or mayonnaise, chopped onion, horseradish, salt, and pepper. Spoon over carrots. Combine cracker crumbs and melted margarine or butter; sprinkle atop casserole. Bake, uncovered, in 350° oven about 30 minutes or till heated through. Makes 4 to 6 servings.

Sweet and Sour Brussels Sprouts

These brussels sprouts have a hearty bacon flavor—

2 9-ounce packages frozen brussels sprouts *or* 3 cups fresh brussels sprouts
4 to 6 slices bacon
2 tablespoons vinegar
2 teaspoons sugar
½ teaspoon salt
¼ teaspoon garlic powder
⅛ teaspoon pepper

Cook frozen brussels sprouts according to package directions. (Or, wash fresh brussels sprouts. Trim stems; remove any wilted or discolored leaves. In covered saucepan cook sprouts in a small amount of boiling salted water for 10 to 15 minutes or till crisp-tender.) Drain.

Meanwhile, in skillet cook bacon till crisp; drain, reserving drippings. Crumble bacon; set aside. To reserved bacon drippings add vinegar, sugar, salt, garlic powder, and pepper. Add brussels sprouts; cook and stir till sprouts are heated through and well coated. Sprinkle with the crumbled bacon. Makes 6 to 8 servings.

Sweet Potato-Pineapple Bake

6 medium sweet potatoes (2 pounds)
¼ cup margarine *or* butter
2 eggs
2 teaspoons finely shredded orange peel (optional)
1 8¼-ounce can pineapple chunks, drained
Orange slices (optional)

Cook sweet potatoes in boiling salted water for 30 to 40 minutes or till tender; drain and peel. Beat potatoes and margarine or butter till fluffy. Beat in eggs, orange peel, and ¾ teaspoon *salt*. Stir in pineapple. Turn into 1-quart casserole. Cover and bake in 325° oven about 45 minutes or till heated through. Garnish with orange slices, if desired. Makes 8 servings.

Vegetables Potpourri

¼ cup chopped onion
1 tablespoon margarine *or* butter
1 cup medium grain rice
1 10-ounce package frozen mixed vegetables *or* one 16-ounce can mixed vegetables, drained
1 10¾-ounce can condensed cream of celery soup
1 cup shredded American cheese *or* process cheese spread (4 ounces)

In skillet cook chopped onion in margarine or butter till tender. Add rice and 2 cups *water*; bring to boiling. Reduce heat; cover and simmer for 5 minutes. Add mixed vegetables, celery soup, and ⅛ teaspoon *pepper*. Cover and simmer 15 minutes more or till rice is tender. Stir in cheese till melted. Makes 6 servings.

Pasta & Rice

For tasty, filling meal-stretchers, remember to include pasta and rice. They contribute to your daily requirements of iron, calcium, and the B vitamins.

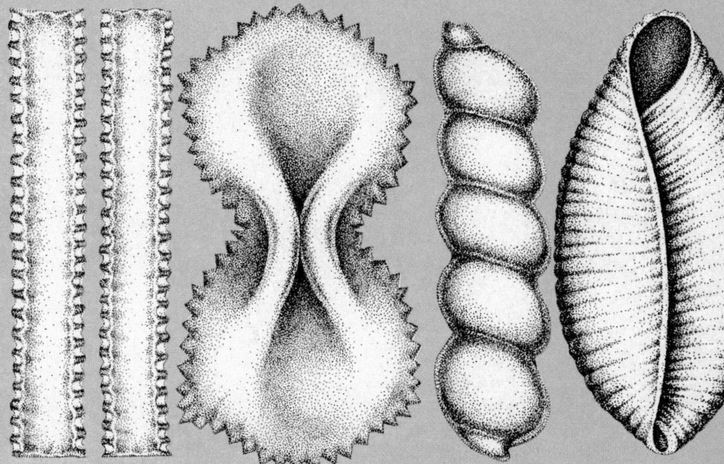

Easy Side Dishes

Try serving pasta or rice as a side dish with a simple fix-up of margarine or butter and your choice of seasonings. Rice can be easily flavored by cooking it in beef or chicken broth rather than water. Plan on 1/2 to 3/4 cup cooked pasta or rice per serving.

Using Pasta

Fancy shapes of pasta may cost slightly more than the common elbow macaroni or plain spaghetti. However, using different shapes of pasta is still one of the least expensive ways to make an ordinary meal seem special. Use your imagination to add variety to that "same old casserole."

Cook pasta in a large amount of boiling salted water just till tender. Since pasta sizes differ, so will cooking times. Drain the cooked pasta, but do not rinse. You'll be washing away valuable nutrients if you do. And, leftover cooked pasta doesn't have to be discarded. Use it in various casseroles and salads.

Rice

Rice comes in several forms, and prices may vary considerably. "Enriched white rice" will appear on the label if vitamins are added to restore nutrients lost in processing. White rice is graded according to grain length. Long grain rice has long, uniform grains that cook up dry and fluffy; reserve it for dishes where appearance counts. Medium and short grain rice are less expensive. Use them in casseroles and puddings. Since the cooked grains stick together more than with long grain rice, you can easily mold them into rice rings, too. Choose white rice according to its use and your budget.

Quick-cooking or precooked rice is the most expensive form—it can cost more than twice as much as regular white rice. Rice mixes, with seasonings added, are generally more expensive than adding your own seasonings to rice at home.

To economize even further, find a use for leftover cooked rice. It makes a tasty addition to meat loaves, casseroles, salads, and sweet puddings.

The following tips will help you prepare perfect white rice every time:

—Use the amount of water specified on the package or in the recipe. If you use too much water, you'll have to drain off the excess—and you'll throw out valuable nutrients, too.

—Cover the pan with a tight-fitting lid, and keep the heat low. This will prevent the rice from overcooking or burning.

—Rice is done when a grain pinched between the thumb and forefinger has no hard core.

Oven Calico Rice

Pictured on pages 60 and 61—

- 1 cup medium grain rice
- ½ cup shredded carrot
- ½ cup chopped celery
- 3 tablespoons snipped parsley
- 2 tablespoons finely chopped onion
- 2 cups water
- 2 tablespoons margarine *or* butter
- 1 tablespoon instant chicken bouillon granules

In a 1½-quart casserole combine rice, carrot, celery, parsley, and onion. In saucepan heat water, margarine or butter, and bouillon granules to boiling. Pour over rice mixture. Cover; bake in 350° oven for 45 to 50 minutes or till rice is tender; stir after 20 minutes. Makes 6 servings.

Onion-Rice Bake

This full-flavored casserole is a perfect accompaniment to beef—

- 1½ teaspoons instant beef bouillon granules
- 1¼ cups boiling water
- 1 10½-ounce can beef consommé
- 1 cup medium grain rice
- ½ cup chopped onion
- 1 2-ounce can mushroom stems and pieces, drained (optional)
- ¼ cup margarine *or* butter, cut up
- Snipped parsley (optional)

In a 1½-quart casserole dissolve bouillon granules in boiling water. Add beef consommé, rice, onion, mushrooms, and margarine or butter. Cover and bake in 350° oven for 50 to 60 minutes or till rice is tender. Garnish with parsley, if desired. Makes 6 servings.

Rice and Spaghetti Pilaf

- ¼ cup margarine *or* butter
- 1 cup medium grain rice
- 2 ounces spaghetti, broken into ¾-inch pieces
- 3 tablespoons finely chopped onion
- 2¾ cups water
- 2 tablespoons instant chicken bouillon granules
- ½ teaspoon dried rosemary *or* thyme, crushed
- Snipped parsley (optional)

In large saucepan melt margarine or butter. Add rice, spaghetti, and onion; cook and stir mixture for 8 to 10 minutes or till spaghetti is golden brown. Add water, bouillon, and rosemary or thyme. Cover; simmer for 25 to 30 minutes or till liquid is absorbed and spaghetti and rice are tender. Season to taste with salt and pepper. Garnish with parsley, if desired. Makes 6 servings.

Broccoli and Cheese Risotto

Risotto is an Italian rice dish; its method of preparation makes it creamy—

- ¼ cup finely chopped onion
- 2 tablespoons margarine *or* butter
- 3 cups water
- 1 cup frozen chopped broccoli
- 1 cup medium grain rice
- 1 tablespoon instant chicken bouillon granules
- ½ teaspoon salt
- Dash pepper
- ½ cup shredded Swiss *or* American cheese *or* process cheese spread (2 ounces)

In medium saucepan cook onion in margarine or butter till onion is tender but not brown. Stir in water, broccoli, rice, bouillon granules, salt, and pepper. Bring to boiling; reduce heat to low. Cover with a tight-fitting lid. Continue cooking for 15 minutes (*do not lift cover*). Remove from heat. Let stand, covered, for 5 to 8 minutes. Rice should be tender but still slightly firm and the mixture should be creamy. Stir cheese into rice mixture just before serving. Makes 6 servings.

Cheese and Rice Casserole

This baked rice dish has a rich custardlike texture—

- ⅓ cup finely chopped celery
- ¼ cup finely chopped onion
- 2 tablespoons margarine *or* butter
- 2 cups cooked rice
- ½ cup shredded American cheese *or* process cheese spread (2 ounces)
- ⅓ cup snipped parsley
- 3 beaten eggs
- 1 cup *reconstituted* nonfat dry milk *or* milk
- ½ teaspoon salt
- ⅛ teaspoon pepper
- Paprika (optional)

Cook celery and onion in margarine or butter till vegetables are tender but not brown. Combine the celery-onion mixture, rice, shredded cheese, and parsley.

In another bowl thoroughly stir together beaten eggs, milk, salt, and pepper; add to the rice mixture. Turn into a 10x6x2-inch baking dish. Place dish in a 13x9x2-inch baking pan on oven rack. Pour hot water into larger pan to depth of 1 inch. Bake in 350° oven for 40 to 45 minutes or till knife inserted just off center comes out clean. Sprinkle with paprika, if desired. Makes 6 to 8 servings.

Breads

Use whole-grain or enriched flour, bread, or cereal in some form at every meal to get needed nutrients at a low cost.

Enriched breads and flour are important for iron and the B vitamins they contribute. Whole grains, especially bran, provide fiber in addition to many nutrients.

Cost-Cutting Tips

Although breads may be the most inexpensive part of your diet, there are still some worthwhile ways to reduce their cost.

—Watch for markdowns on day-old bread and baked goods in your grocery store and at bakery outlet stores. If you have room, buy now and freeze for later.

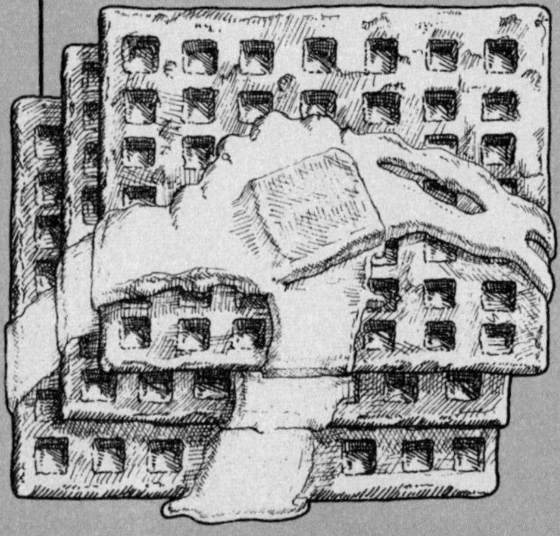

—You may be able to cut costs on basic ingredients you frequently use. Look for a store brand or generic brand of flour, sugar, and other baking goods. These are often cheaper than national brands.

Making Sour Milk

When you don't have buttermilk on hand, substitute an equal amount of "soured" milk for the buttermilk. Combine 1 tablespoon *lemon juice or vinegar* and enough *milk* to make *1 cup* total liquid. Let stand 5 minutes before using.

Making Croutons

Don't discard stale bread. Use it to make croutons. Although white bread is most often used, add variety with whole wheat, rye, or any other yeast bread. To make croutons, brush bread slices lightly with melted *margarine*; cut into ½-inch cubes. Spread in shallow baking pan; sprinkle with *garlic powder* or your choice of crushed *dried herbs*, if desired. Bake in 350° oven about 30 minutes or till bread

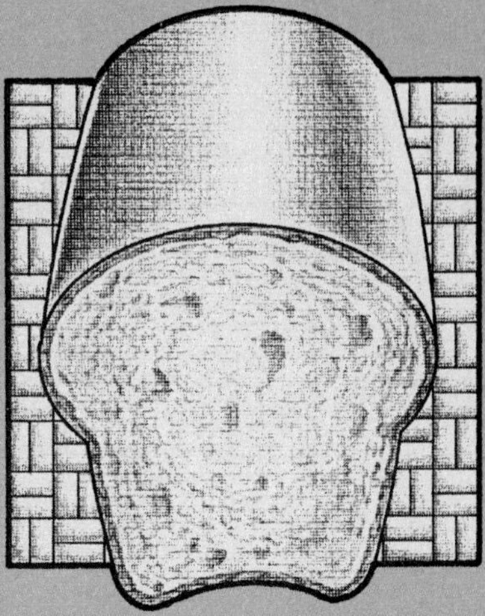

cubes are dry and golden; stir at least once during baking. Cool; store in covered container in refrigerator. (Each slice of bread yields about ¾ cup croutons.)

Making Bread Crumbs

To make fine dry bread crumbs, oven-toast stale bread slices in 300° oven till crisp and dry. Place bread slices in a blender container; cover and process till finely crushed. Or, place toasted bread in a plastic bag and crush to fine crumbs.

For seasoned bread crumbs, mix 1 cup fine dry *bread crumbs*, 1 teaspoon *salt*, ½ teaspoon *garlic salt*, ¼ teaspoon *paprika*, and ¼ teaspoon dried *thyme*, crushed. Cover; store bread crumbs in cool dry place. Use either seasoned or unseasoned dry bread crumbs in meat loaves, for coatings, and to sprinkle over casseroles for a crispy topping.

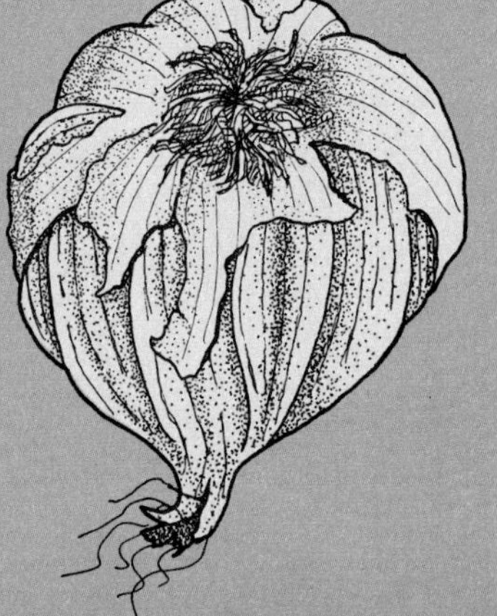

Homemade Biscuit Mix

- 10 cups all-purpose flour
- 1/3 cup baking powder
- 1/4 cup sugar
- 2 cups shortening that does not require refrigeration

In large bowl stir together flour, baking powder, sugar, and 4 teaspoons *salt*. With pastry blender cut in shortening till mixture resembles coarse crumbs. Store in covered airtight container up to six weeks at room temperature. To use, spoon mix lightly into measuring cup; level off with a straight-edged spatula. (For longer storage, place in sealed freezer container; store in freezer up to six months. To use, allow mix to come to room temperature.) Makes 12½ cups.

Biscuits: Place 2 cups *Homemade Biscuit Mix* in a bowl; make a well in center. Add ½ cup *reconstituted nonfat dry milk or milk*. Stir with fork just till dough follows fork around bowl. On lightly floured surface, knead dough 10 to 12 strokes. Roll or pat to ½-inch thickness. Cut dough with floured 2½-inch biscuit cutter. Bake on baking sheet in 450° oven 10 to 12 minutes. Makes 10.

Muffins: Combine 3 cups *Homemade Biscuit Mix* and 3 tablespoons *sugar*. Mix 1 beaten *egg* and 1 cup *reconstituted nonfat dry milk or milk*; add all at once to dry ingredients. Stir till moistened. Fill greased muffin cups ⅔ full. Bake in 400° oven for 20 to 25 minutes or till golden. Makes 12.

Pancakes: Place 2 cups *Homemade Biscuit Mix* in a bowl. Add 2 beaten *eggs* and 1 cup *reconstituted nonfat dry milk or milk* all at once to biscuit mix, stirring till blended but still slightly lumpy. For each pancake pour about ¼ cup batter onto hot, lightly greased griddle. Cook till golden brown, turning to cook other side. Makes 10.

Pumpkin-Spice Loaves

- 4 cups all-purpose flour
- 4 teaspoons baking powder
- 1 teaspoon salt
- 1 teaspoon ground cinnamon
- 1/2 teaspoon baking soda
- 1/4 teaspoon ground cloves
- 2 cups sugar
- 2/3 cup shortening
- 4 eggs
- 1 16-ounce can (2 cups) pumpkin
- 1/2 cup *reconstituted* nonfat dry milk *or* milk
- 1/2 cup chopped nuts (optional)

Combine flour, baking powder, salt, cinnamon, soda, and cloves; set aside. In large mixer bowl cream together sugar, shortening, and eggs. Add pumpkin and milk; beat till smooth. Mix in dry ingredients. Add nuts, if desired. Turn batter into two greased and floured 8x4x2-inch *or* 9x5x3-inch loaf pans. Bake in 350° oven for 55 to 60 minutes or till done. Cool on wire rack. Makes 2 loaves.

Spiced Carrot-Bran Muffins

Shredded carrot adds color and moistness to these bran muffins—

- 1 cup whole bran cereal
- 1 cup buttermilk *or* sour milk (see tip, page 72)
- 1 cup all-purpose flour
- 1/4 cup packed brown sugar
- 2 teaspoons baking powder
- 3/4 teaspoon ground cinnamon *or* allspice
- 1/2 teaspoon baking soda
- 1/2 teaspoon salt
- 1 beaten egg
- 2 medium carrots, finely shredded (¾ cup)
- 3 tablespoons cooking oil

In bowl combine bran and buttermilk or sour milk; let stand about 3 minutes or till liquid is absorbed.

In mixing bowl stir together flour, brown sugar, baking powder, cinnamon or allspice, baking soda, and salt. Make a well in the center of dry ingredients. Combine cereal-milk mixture, beaten egg, shredded carrot, and cooking oil; add all at once to dry ingredients, stirring just till moistened (batter will be thick). Fill greased *or* paper bake cup-lined muffin pans ⅔ full. Bake in 400° oven for 15 to 20 minutes or till muffins are golden brown. Makes 12 muffins.

Whole Wheat-Apple Muffins

Serve these muffins fresh from the oven for breakfast, lunch, or dinner—

- 1½ cups whole wheat flour
- 1/2 cup all-purpose flour
- 2½ teaspoons baking powder
- 3/4 teaspoon salt
- 1 beaten egg
- 3/4 cup *reconstituted* nonfat dry milk *or* milk
- 1/3 cup cooking oil
- 1/3 cup honey
- 1 cup chopped apple

In mixing bowl stir together whole wheat flour, all-purpose flour, baking powder, and salt. Make a well in the center of dry ingredients. Combine beaten egg, milk, cooking oil, and honey. Add egg mixture all at once to dry ingredients, stirring just till dry ingredients are moistened. Batter should be lumpy. Fold in chopped apple.

Spoon batter into greased or paper bake cup-lined muffin pans, filling each about ¾ full. Bake in 400° oven for 18 to 20 minutes or till muffins are golden brown. Makes about 12 muffins.

Banana Nut Bread

- 1¾ cups all-purpose flour
- 1¼ teaspoons baking powder
- ¾ teaspoon salt
- ½ teaspoon baking soda
- ⅔ cup sugar
- ⅓ cup shortening
- 2 eggs
- 2 tablespoons *reconstituted* nonfat dry milk *or* milk
- 1 cup mashed ripe banana
- ¼ cup chopped nuts

In mixing bowl stir together flour, baking powder, salt, and baking soda; set aside.

In mixer bowl cream sugar and shortening with electric mixer till light, scraping sides of bowl often. Add eggs, one at a time, and the milk, beating till smooth and fluffy after each addition. Add flour mixture and mashed banana alternately to creamed mixture, beating till smooth after each addition. Gently fold in the chopped nuts.

Turn batter into lightly greased 8x4x2-inch loaf pan. Bake in 350° oven for 60 to 65 minutes or till wooden pick inserted near center comes out clean. Cool bread in pan 10 minutes. Remove from pan; cool thoroughly on wire rack. For easier slicing, wrap bread in foil and store overnight. Makes 1 loaf.

Basic Crepes

- 1 cup all-purpose flour
- 1½ cups *reconstituted* nonfat dry milk *or* milk
- 2 eggs
- 1 tablespoon cooking oil
- ¼ teaspoon salt

In mixer bowl combine flour, milk, eggs, cooking oil, and salt; beat with an electric mixer or rotary beater till blended. Heat a lightly greased 6-inch skillet. Remove from heat; spoon in about 2 tablespoons batter. Lift and tilt skillet to spread batter evenly. Return to heat; brown on one side only. (Or, cook crepes on an inverted crepe pan according to manufacturer's directions.) To remove crepe, invert pan over paper toweling; loosen crepe with spatula. Repeat cooking with the remaining batter, greasing skillet occasionally. Makes 16 to 18.

Bacon-and-Cheese Oven Pancake

- 6 slices bacon
- 1 cup all-purpose flour
- 2 tablespoons sugar
- 1 tablespoon baking powder
- ½ teaspoon salt
- 1 egg
- ¾ cup *reconstituted* nonfat dry milk *or* milk
- 1 cup shredded American cheese *or* process cheese spread (4 ounces)
- Margarine *or* butter
- Maple-flavored syrup

In skillet cook bacon till crisp; drain, reserving 3 tablespoons drippings. Crumble bacon and set aside. In mixer bowl stir together flour, sugar, baking powder, and salt. Combine egg, milk, and reserved bacon drippings; add all at once to dry ingredients, beating with electric mixer or rotary beater till smooth. Stir in crumbled bacon.

Spread batter evenly in greased and floured 15x10x1-inch baking pan. Bake in 425° oven for 15 minutes. Sprinkle with shredded cheese; bake 2 to 3 minutes more or till cheese is melted. Cut into squares. Pass margarine or butter and maple-flavored syrup. Makes 4 to 6 servings.

Peach Crumb Coffee Cake

- 1 16-ounce can peach slices
- 2 tablespoons cold water
- 2 tablespoons cornstarch
- 2 cups all-purpose flour
- 1 cup sugar
- 2 teaspoons baking powder
- ½ teaspoon salt
- ½ cup margarine *or* butter
- 1 egg
- ¾ cup *reconstituted* nonfat dry milk *or* milk
- ½ cup all-purpose flour
- ½ cup sugar
- ½ teaspoon ground cinnamon *or* allspice
- ¼ cup margarine *or* butter

Drain peaches, reserving syrup. Chop peaches; place chopped peaches and reserved syrup in saucepan. Blend together water and cornstarch; stir into peaches and syrup. Cook and stir over medium heat till thickened and bubbly. Remove from heat; set aside.

In mixing bowl combine the 2 cups flour, 1 cup sugar, the baking powder, and salt. Cut in ½ cup margarine or butter till mixture resembles coarse crumbs. Place egg in 2-cup liquid measure; add enough of the ¾ cup milk to measure *1 cup* liquid. Lightly beat egg and milk together. Add to dry ingredients, mixing well.

Spread batter in greased 13x9x2-inch baking pan. Top with thickened peach mixture. Stir together remaining ½ cup flour, ½ cup sugar, and the cinnamon or allspice; cut in ¼ cup margarine or butter till mixture resembles coarse crumbs.

Sprinkle crumb-spice mixture over peach layer. Bake in 400° oven for 30 to 35 minutes or till golden. Cut into squares. Serve warm. Makes 1 coffee cake.

Whole Wheat and Bran Rolls

Pictured on pages 60 and 61—

1½ cups whole wheat flour
1 package active dry yeast
1 cup *reconstituted* nonfat dry milk *or* milk
¼ cup shortening
3 tablespoons sugar
1 teaspoon salt
1 egg
⅓ cup whole bran cereal
1 cup all-purpose flour

In large mixer bowl stir together whole wheat flour and yeast. In saucepan heat milk, shortening, sugar, and salt just till warm (115° to 120°) and shortening is almost melted; stir constantly. Add to flour mixture; add egg. Beat at low speed of electric mixer for ½ minute, scraping sides of bowl constantly. Beat for 3 minutes at high speed.

Stir in bran and the all-purpose flour. Place dough in a lightly greased bowl; turn once to grease surface. Cover and chill at least 1½ hours.

Shape dough into 18 balls. Place in greased muffin cups. Cover; let rise till double (about 1¼ hours). Bake in 400° oven about 12 minutes. Makes 18 rolls.

Cheese Bread

3½ to 4 cups all-purpose flour
1 package active dry yeast
1¼ cups water
1½ cups shredded American *or* Swiss cheese *or* process cheese spread (6 ounces)
¼ cup sugar
1½ teaspoons salt
1 egg

In large mixer bowl combine *1½ cups* of the flour and the yeast. In saucepan heat water, shredded cheese, sugar, and salt just till warm (115° to 120°), stirring constantly. Add to flour mixture; add egg. Beat at low speed of electric mixer for ½ minute, scraping sides of bowl constantly. Beat for 3 minutes at high speed. Stir in as much of the remaining flour as you can mix in using a spoon. Turn out onto lightly floured surface. Knead in enough of the remaining flour to make a moderately stiff dough that is smooth and elastic (knead 6 to 8 minutes total). Shape into a ball. Place in lightly greased bowl; turn once. Cover; let rise in warm place till double (1 to 1¼ hours).

Punch down; divide in half. Cover; let rest 10 minutes. Shape into two loaves; place in 2 greased 8x4x2-inch loaf pans. Cover; let rise till nearly double (about 45 minutes). Bake in 350° oven for 40 to 45 minutes. Cover with foil the last 20 minutes to prevent overbrowning. Remove from pans; cool on wire rack. Makes 2 loaves.

Frosted Banana Rolls

4¾ cups to 5¼ cups all-purpose flour
2 packages active dry yeast
1 cup *reconstituted* nonfat dry milk *or* milk
¼ cup granulated sugar
¼ cup margarine *or* butter
1 egg
1 cup mashed ripe banana
1 teaspoon vanilla
⅓ cup granulated sugar
¾ cup chopped nuts (optional)
¼ cup margarine *or* butter, melted
¾ teaspoon ground allspice *or* cinnamon
2 cups sifted powdered sugar
3 tablespoons *reconstituted* nonfat dry milk *or* milk

In large mixer bowl stir together *2 cups* of the flour and the yeast. In saucepan heat 1 cup milk, ¼ cup granulated sugar, ¼ cup margarine or butter, and 1 teaspoon *salt* till just warm (115° to 120°) and margarine is almost melted; stir constantly. Add to dry ingredients in bowl. Add egg, mashed banana, and vanilla. Beat at low speed of electric mixer for ½ minute, scraping sides of bowl constantly. Beat for 3 minutes at high speed.

Stir in as much of the remaining flour as you can mix in using a spoon. Turn out onto lightly floured surface. Knead in enough of the remaining flour to make a moderately soft dough that is smooth and elastic (3 to 5 minutes total). Shape into a ball.

Place dough in lightly greased bowl; turn once to grease surface. Cover; let dough rise in warm place till double (about 40 minutes). Punch down; divide dough in half. Cover and let rest for 10 minutes.

Roll each piece of dough to a 16x9-inch rectangle. Combine ⅓ cup granulated sugar, chopped nuts, ¼ cup melted margarine or butter, and the allspice or cinnamon. Spread each rectangle with *half* of the sugar and nut mixture. Roll up jelly-roll style, beginning from long side; seal edges and ends. Cut each roll of dough into 16 pieces. Place rolls on greased baking sheets. Cover; let rise till nearly double (about 30 minutes). Bake in 375° oven for 15 to 18 minutes or till rolls are golden.

For glaze, combine powdered sugar and 3 tablespoons milk. Add additional milk, if necessary, to make of good drizzling consistency. Drizzle glaze over warm rolls. Sprinkle rolls with additional chopped nuts, if desired. Makes 36.

Desserts

Dessert doesn't have to be only a luxury if you plan it as part of the total meal. You can still serve desserts and stay within your budget by not using expensive ingredients. Make dessert a nutritious part of the meal, and satisfy your sweet tooth as well.

Nutritious Desserts

Nutritious dessert ideas aren't difficult to think up. For example, provide part of the day's milk requirement by serving a custard or cream pudding or pie. Add vitamins with a fruit dessert. Likewise, a dessert containing eggs or peanut butter adds protein.

Leftovers For Dessert

Even leftovers can be the beginning of a tasty dessert. Day-old bread can be the start of a warm and homey bread pudding. Or, use leftover cooked rice in a creamy rice pudding. Add leftover or small amounts of fruit (fresh, frozen, or canned) to sauces, fruit compotes, cobblers, upside down cakes, shortcakes, and parfaits.

And don't forget to save the syrup from canned or frozen fruits. Thicken the syrup with cornstarch for delectable dessert sauces. The syrup also can be used in place of part of the water in gelatin-based desserts.

When you use oranges (or lemons) in a recipe, don't discard the peel; reserve and finely shred it. Freeze the shredded peel in a tightly sealed container so it's handy for use in main dish, dessert, and bread recipes.

Homemade Versus Store-Bought

Also consider the cost of homemade versus store-bought dessert items. Watch for sales on cake, brownie, and pudding mixes. On sale, the packaged mix may be less expensive than making desserts from scratch. However, frozen prepared cakes, brownies, pies, and pie crusts are usually more costly than your own homemade version.

A perfect tender and flaky pie crust is unbeatable when made from scratch. It costs less to make

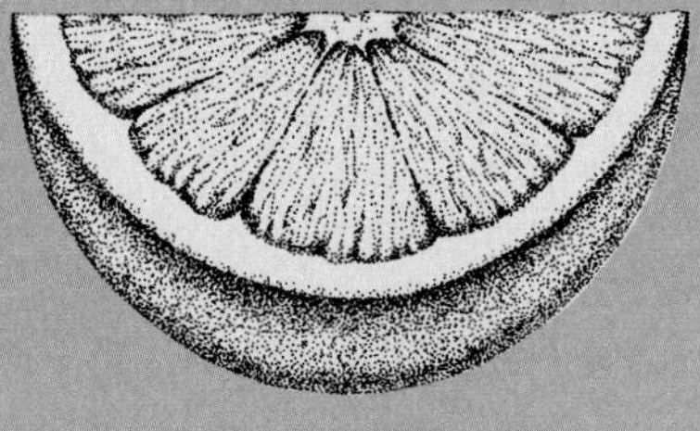

your own than to buy pie crust mixes or the frozen ready-to-bake crusts. If the convenience of frozen pie crusts is important to you, make several pie crusts at one time. Wrap them, unbaked, in moisture-vaporproof wrap and freeze for up to 2 months. You'll have pie crusts on hand for a variety of fillings.

Instead of whipped cream or whipped topping, try dolloping desserts with Lemony Whipped Topping (see recipe, page 77). Not only is it less costly, but it adds nutritional value to desserts.

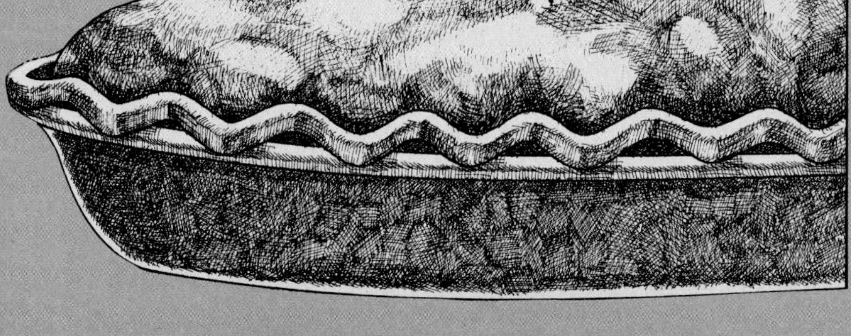

Lemony Whipped Topping

Dollop this fluffy topping on fruits, cakes, pies, and other desserts—

- 2/3 cup nonfat dry milk *powder*
- 1/3 cup ice water
- 1/4 cup sugar
- 3 tablespoons lemon juice

Chill small mixer bowl and beaters. In the chilled bowl combine nonfat dry milk powder and ice water. Beat at medium speed of electric mixer for 5 minutes or till soft peaks form. Add sugar and lemon juice. Continue beating about 2 minutes more or till stiff peaks form. Use topping immediately. Makes about 2 cups.

Single-Crust Pastry

- 1 1/4 cups all-purpose flour
- 1/2 teaspoon salt
- 1/3 cup shortening *or* lard
- 3 to 4 tablespoons cold water

Stir together flour and salt. Cut in shortening till pieces are the size of small peas. Sprinkle *1 tablespoon* of the water over part of mixture; gently toss with fork. Push to side of bowl. Repeat till all is moistened. Form dough into a ball.

On lightly floured surface roll dough into a 12-inch circle. Wrap pastry around rolling pin. Unroll onto a 9-inch pie plate. Ease pastry into plate; flute edge.

For a baked pie shell, prick bottom and sides of pastry with fork. Bake in 450° oven for 10 to 12 minutes. (Or, line pastry with foil and fill with dry beans, or line pastry with a double thickness of heavy-duty foil. Bake in 450° oven 5 minutes. Remove beans and foil or heavy-duty foil; bake 5 to 7 minutes more or till golden.) Makes one 9-inch pastry shell.

Pineapple-Custard Mold

- 1/2 cup sugar
- 1 envelope unflavored gelatin
- 1/4 teaspoon salt
- 3/4 cup *reconstituted* nonfat dry milk *or* milk
- 2 slightly beaten egg yolks
- 1 teaspoon vanilla
- 1/2 cup evaporated milk
- 2 egg whites
- 2 tablespoons sugar
- 1 8 1/4-ounce can crushed pineapple
- 2 tablespoons sugar
- 4 teaspoons cornstarch
- Dash salt
- 3/4 cup orange juice

In saucepan combine the 1/2 cup sugar, unflavored gelatin, and the 1/4 teaspoon salt. Stir in milk and egg yolks. Cook and stir till slightly thickened. Remove from heat; add vanilla. Chill till partially set, stirring occasionally.

Meanwhile, pour evaporated milk into shallow pan. Freeze till edges are icy; whip till stiff peaks form. Fold into gelatin mixture. With electric mixer beat egg whites till soft peaks form; gradually add the 2 tablespoons sugar, beating till stiff peaks form. Fold beaten egg whites into gelatin mixture. Turn into 4 1/2-cup mold; chill 6 hours or overnight.

To prepare sauce, drain pineapple, reserving liquid. In saucepan combine 2 tablespoons sugar, the cornstarch, and dash salt. Stir in reserved pineapple liquid and orange juice. Cook and stir till thickened and bubbly. Reduce heat; cook 1 minute more. Cool slightly; stir in pineapple. Chill.

To serve, unmold gelatin; top with sauce. Makes 8 servings.

Individual Chocolate Pies

Pictured on pages 60 and 61—

- Pastry for Single-Crust Pie (see recipe, left)
- 2 eggs
- 1 4-serving-size package *regular* chocolate pudding mix
- 2 cups *reconstituted* nonfat dry milk *or* milk
- 1/2 teaspoon vanilla
- 1/4 teaspoon cream of tartar
- 1/4 cup sugar

Prepare pastry dough as directed. Roll to 1/8-inch thickness; cut into twelve 3 1/2-inch circles; reroll dough as necessary. Place pastry circles on baking sheet; prick with tines of fork. Bake in 450° oven for 6 to 8 minutes or till golden. Cool.

Separate eggs; set whites aside for meringue. Lightly beat yolks with fork. In medium heavy saucepan cook pudding mix according to package directions, using the 2 cups milk. Remove from heat; stir about *1 cup* of the thickened chocolate pudding mixture into beaten yolks. Return all to saucepan; bring to boiling. Cook and stir 2 minutes more. Remove from heat; cover surface of pudding with plastic wrap or waxed paper. Cool.

In small mixer bowl beat egg whites, vanilla, and cream of tartar with electric mixer till soft peaks form. Gradually add sugar; beat till stiff and glossy peaks form.

To assemble, place one pastry circle on baking sheet. Spread with about *2 tablespoons* of the chocolate filling. Top with another pastry circle; spread with 2 tablespoons more filling. Repeat to make 5 more stacks, using 2 pastry circles for each stack. Spread some meringue on top of each pudding stack. Broil 4 to 5 inches from heat for 1 to 2 minutes or till golden. Makes 6 servings.

Orange Meringue Pie

Try using reconstituted frozen orange juice concentrate instead of fresh juice in this luscious orange pie—

- Single-Crust Pastry (see recipe, page 77)
- 3/4 cup sugar
- 1/4 cup cornstarch
- 1/4 teaspoon salt
- 1 1/2 teaspoons finely shredded orange peel (optional; set aside)
- 2 cups orange juice
- 3 slightly beaten egg yolks
- 2 tablespoons margarine *or* butter
- 3 egg whites
- 1/2 teaspoon vanilla
- 1/4 teaspoon cream of tartar
- 1/3 cup sugar

Prepare and roll out pastry; fit into a 9-inch pie plate. Trim and flute edge; prick pastry. Bake in 450° oven for 10 to 12 minutes or till golden. Cool on wire rack.

In saucepan combine the 3/4 cup sugar, the cornstarch, and salt. Gradually stir in the orange juice. Cook and stir over medium-high heat till thickened and bubbly. Reduce heat; cook and stir 2 minutes more. Remove from heat. Slowly stir about *1 cup* of the hot mixture into the beaten yolks. Immediately return mixture to saucepan. Cook and stir 2 minutes more. Remove from heat; stir in margarine or butter. Stir in orange peel, if desired. Turn hot filling into baked pastry shell.

For meringue, in mixer bowl beat egg whites, vanilla, and cream of tartar with rotary beater or electric mixer till soft peaks form. Gradually add the 1/3 cup sugar, beating till stiff peaks form. Immediately spread meringue over hot orange filling; seal to edge. Bake in 350° oven for 12 to 15 minutes or till meringue is golden. Cool before serving. Cover; chill to store.

Caramel Custard Pie

- Single-Crust Pastry (see recipe, page 77)
- 4 eggs
- 1 13-ounce can *and* one 5 1/3-ounce can evaporated milk (2 cups total)
- 1 cup packed brown sugar

Prepare and roll out pastry. Fit into a 9-inch pie plate. Trim pastry to 1/2 inch beyond edge. Flute edge high; do not prick. Bake in 450° oven for 5 minutes. Cool on wire rack.

For filling, in mixing bowl beat eggs slightly. Stir in the evaporated milk and brown sugar, stirring thoroughly to dissolve brown sugar. Place pie shell on oven rack; pour mixture into the partially baked pastry shell. To prevent overbrowning, cover edge of pie with foil. Bake in 350° oven for 25 minutes. Remove foil; bake for 20 to 25 minutes more or till knife inserted near center comes out clean. Cool thoroughly on rack. Cover; chill to store.

Note: The surface of this pie will typically appear mottled and bubbly.

Surprise Pie

Rolled oats and coconut are the surprises in this pie filling—

- Single-Crust Pastry (see recipe, page 77)
- 1/2 cup sugar
- 1/4 cup margarine *or* butter, softened
- 1 cup light corn syrup
- 1/4 teaspoon salt
- 3 eggs
- 1/2 cup flaked coconut
- 1/2 cup quick-cooking rolled oats

Prepare and roll out pastry; fit into a 9-inch pie plate. Trim pastry to 1/2 inch beyond edge of pie plate. Flute edge; do not prick pastry. Bake in 450° oven for 5 minutes. Cool on rack.

In mixer bowl gradually add sugar to softened margarine or butter, beating till fluffy with rotary beater or electric mixer. Add corn syrup and salt; beat well. Add eggs, one at a time, beating till thoroughly mixed. Stir in coconut and rolled oats.

Place pie shell on oven rack; pour filling into the partially baked pastry shell. To prevent overbrowning, cover edge of pie with foil. Bake in 350° oven for 30 minutes. Remove foil, bake for 15 to 20 minutes more or till knife inserted near center comes out clean. Cool before serving. Cover; chill to store.

Individual Orange-Coconut Flans

- 1/2 cup flaked coconut
- 5 eggs
- 1/2 teaspoon salt
- 1/2 cup sugar
- 2 cups *reconstituted* nonfat dry milk *or* milk
- 2 tablespoons frozen orange juice concentrate, thawed

Toast coconut in 325° oven about 15 minutes or till golden brown. Set aside to cool. In large mixing bowl beat eggs and salt till blended. Add sugar. Gradually stir in milk and orange juice concentrate. Stir in toasted coconut. Pour mixture into eight 6-ounce custard cups. Set cups in a large baking pan; place on oven rack. Pour boiling water around cups in baking pan to a depth of 1 inch.

Bake in 325° oven for 50 to 55 minutes or till knife inserted near center comes out clean. Chill thoroughly. Unmold the flans on serving dishes or serve in the custard cups. Makes 8 servings.

Broiled Banana Crisp

4 small bananas
1 tablespoon lemon juice
3 tablespoons brown sugar
3 tablespoons quick-cooking rolled oats
2 tablespoons all-purpose flour
1/4 teaspoon ground cinnamon
1/8 teaspoon ground nutmeg
2 tablespoons margarine *or* butter
Vanilla ice cream *or* ice milk

Peel bananas; cut in half lengthwise, then in half crosswise. Drizzle lemon juice over bananas. Place bananas in 4 individual broiler-proof dishes.

In mixing bowl combine brown sugar, rolled oats, flour, cinnamon, and nutmeg. Cut in margarine or butter till mixture is crumbly. Sprinkle mixture over bananas. Place under broiler 4 to 5 inches from heat. Broil for 3 to 4 minutes or till mixture is golden and bubbly. Before serving, top with ice cream or ice milk. Makes 4 servings.

Pudding and Fruit Parfaits

Try other canned fruits, too—

1 16-ounce can peach slices *or* one 17-ounce can fruit cocktail
2 tablespoons sugar
1 tablespoon cornstarch
1/8 teaspoon ground nutmeg
Dash salt
1 4-serving-size package *instant* vanilla *or* lemon pudding mix
1 cup *reconstituted* nonfat dry milk *or* milk
1 cup dairy sour cream *or* plain yogurt

Drain peaches or fruit cocktail, reserving syrup. Cut peach slices into bite-sized pieces. In saucepan combine sugar, cornstarch, nutmeg, and salt. Gradually stir in reserved fruit syrup. Cook, stirring constantly, till mixture is thickened and bubbly; cook 1 minute more. Stir in peaches or fruit cocktail; cool.

Prepare pudding mix according to package directions *except* substitute the 1 cup milk and 1 cup sour cream or yogurt for the milk called for. Let stand for 10 minutes. In parfait glasses alternately layer pudding and the fruit mixture, beginning with pudding and ending with fruit mixture. Chill till serving time. Makes 6 servings.

Peanut Butter Cupcakes

3 tablespoons brown sugar
3 tablespoons all-purpose flour
2 tablespoons peanut butter
1 tablespoon margarine *or* butter, melted
1/4 cup peanut butter
3 tablespoons shortening
3/4 cup packed brown sugar
1 egg
1 cup all-purpose flour
1 teaspoon baking powder
1/4 teaspoon salt
1/4 teaspoon ground cinnamon
1/2 cup *reconstituted* nonfat dry milk *or* milk

For peanut butter topping, combine the 3 tablespoons brown sugar, 3 tablespoons flour, 2 tablespoons peanut butter, and the margarine or butter till mixture is crumbly; set aside.

Cream together the 1/4 cup peanut butter, the shortening, and the 3/4 cup brown sugar till light and fluffy, scraping sides of bowl frequently. Add egg; beat till fluffy. Stir together the 1 cup flour, the baking powder, salt, and cinnamon. Add dry ingredients to the creamed mixture alternately with the milk, beating well after each addition.

Spoon into greased or paper bake cup-lined muffin cups, filling each 1/2 full. Top with crumbly peanut butter mixture. Bake in 375° oven for 20 to 25 minutes or till done. Makes 12 cupcakes.

Apple-Cranberry Crisp

1 1/2 cups chunk-style applesauce
1/4 cup packed brown sugar
2 tablespoons all-purpose flour
1 tablespoon lemon juice
1 16-ounce can whole cranberry sauce
1 cup quick-cooking rolled oats
1/2 cup all-purpose flour
1/2 cup packed brown sugar
1/2 teaspoon ground cinnamon *or* nutmeg
1/2 cup margarine *or* butter
Reconstituted nonfat dry milk *or* milk (optional)

In saucepan combine applesauce, the 1/4 cup brown sugar, the 2 tablespoons flour, and the lemon juice. Cook and stir till thickened and bubbly. Stir in cranberry sauce; heat through. Set aside.

In mixing bowl combine oats, the 1/2 cup flour, the 1/2 cup brown sugar, cinnamon or nutmeg, and 1/4 teaspoon *salt*. Cut in margarine or butter till mixture is crumbly. Press *half* of the oat mixture into bottom of 8x8x2-inch baking pan. Spread applesauce-cranberry mixture over oat layer; sprinkle with remaining oat mixture. Bake in 375° oven about 35 minutes or till golden brown. Serve warm or cooled spooned into individual dishes. Serve with milk, if desired. Makes 9 servings.

Lemon Yogurt-Raspberry Tarts

2 cups all-purpose flour
1 teaspoon salt
⅔ cup shortening *or* lard
6 to 7 tablespoons cold water
1 3-ounce package lemon-flavored gelatin
2 tablespoons sugar
1¼ cups boiling water
1 cup lemon yogurt
½ of a 10-ounce jar (about ½ cup) raspberry *or* strawberry jelly

For tart shells, in mixing bowl stir together flour and salt. Cut in shortening or lard till pieces are the size of small peas. Sprinkle *1 tablespoon* of the water over part of the mixture; gently toss with a fork. Push to side of bowl. Repeat till all is moistened. Divide pastry in half.

On lightly floured surface roll *half* of the pastry at a time to ⅛-inch thickness. Cut out three 5-inch circles from each half of pastry. Fit pastry circles over inverted 6-ounce custard cups, pinching pleats at intervals to fit around the cups; prick with a fork. Bake in 450° oven 12 to 15 minutes or till golden. Cool.

For filling, in mixing bowl combine the lemon-flavored gelatin and sugar; add the boiling water, stirring till gelatin is dissolved. Beat in the lemon yogurt. Chill gelatin mixture till partially set (the consistency of unbeaten egg whites). Beat the gelatin mixture with rotary beater or electric mixer for 1 to 2 minutes or till light and fluffy. Chill till mixture mounds when spooned. Spoon filling into baked tart shells. Cover; chill several hours or overnight till set. Heat jelly just till warm; spoon over tarts. Garnish with lemon peel twists, if desired. Makes 6 tarts.

Baked Rice Pudding

Dress up this warm and homey pudding by decorating with cinnamon or nutmeg—

2 cups *reconstituted* nonfat dry milk *or* milk
½ cup medium grain rice
½ cup raisins (optional)
¼ cup margarine *or* butter
1½ cups nonfat dry milk *powder*
⅓ cup sugar
½ teaspoon salt
2 cups water
1½ teaspoons vanilla
3 beaten eggs
Ground cinnamon *or* nutmeg
Raisins (optional)
Reconstituted nonfat dry milk *or* milk (optional)

In saucepan bring the 2 cups milk, the rice, and ½ cup raisins to boiling; reduce heat. Cover and simmer over very low heat about 20 minutes or till rice is tender. Remove from heat; stir in margarine or butter till melted.

Combine nonfat dry milk powder, sugar, and salt. Stir in water and vanilla, mixing till milk powder is dissolved. Stir in beaten eggs. Gradually stir hot rice mixture into egg mixture. Pour into a 2-quart casserole. Place casserole in a 13x9x2-inch baking pan on oven rack. Carefully pour boiling water around casserole in pan to depth of 1 inch. Bake in 325° oven for 35 minutes; stir. Sprinkle with cinnamon or nutmeg in decorative fashion. Arrange additional raisins atop, if desired. Bake 25 to 30 minutes more or till knife inserted near center comes out clean. Let stand about 20 minutes before serving. (Or, cover and chill before serving.) Serve with additional milk, if desired. Makes 6 servings.

Pineapple-Filled Dessert Crepes

The fluffy pineapple filling makes these crepes an elegant dessert—

⅓ cup sugar
2 tablespoons cornstarch
¼ teaspoon salt
1 20-ounce can crushed pineapple
1 tablespoon lemon juice
3 slightly beaten egg yolks
3 egg whites
¼ teaspoon cream of tartar
16 Basic Crepes (see recipe, page 74)
Sifted powdered sugar

For filling, in saucepan combine sugar, cornstarch, and salt. Stir in *undrained* pineapple and lemon juice; mix well. Cook and stir over medium heat till thickened and bubbly. Reduce heat; cook and stir for 2 minutes more. Remove from heat.

Gradually stir about *1 cup* of the hot pineapple mixture into the beaten egg yolks. Return mixture to saucepan; cook and stir for 2 minutes more. Pour into bowl. Place clear plastic wrap or waxed paper directly on top of filling; smooth wrap or paper to touch side of bowl. Cool.

In mixer bowl beat egg whites and cream of tartar using rotary beater or electric mixer till stiff peaks form. Gently fold in the cooled pineapple mixture.

Spread about 3 tablespoons of the pineapple filling over unbrowned side of each crepe, leaving ¼-inch rim around edge. Roll up crepe jelly-roll style. Repeat with remaining crepes. Serve immediately or cover and chill. Sprinkle with powdered sugar before serving. Makes 8 servings.

Baked Rice Pudding and *Lemon Yogurt-Raspberry Tarts* are desserts family and friends will love. ▶

Cream Puffs

Try these with the filling from Pineapple-Filled Dessert Crepes on page 80—

½ cup margarine *or* butter
1 cup water
1 cup all-purpose flour
4 eggs

In medium saucepan melt margarine or butter. Add water; bring to boiling. Add flour and ¼ teaspoon *salt* all at once; stir vigorously. Cook and stir till mixture forms a ball that doesn't separate. Remove from heat; cool about 5 minutes. Add eggs, one at a time; beat with wooden spoon after each addition for 1 to 2 minutes or till smooth. Drop batter by heaping tablespoonfuls 3 inches apart onto greased baking sheet. Bake in 400° oven about 30 minutes or till golden brown and puffy. Remove from oven. Split; remove soft dough from inside. Cool on wire rack. Fill with desired filling, pudding, or fruit mixture. Makes 10.

Pumpkin Dessert Soufflé

Use any leftover canned pumpkin for Pumpkin-Streusel Coffee Cake (see recipe, page 89)—

1 cup evaporated milk
⅔ cup packed brown sugar
2 envelopes unflavored gelatin
1½ cups canned pumpkin
3 slightly beaten egg yolks
½ teaspoon ground cinnamon
½ teaspoon ground nutmeg
¼ teaspoon ground ginger
3 egg whites
⅓ cup granulated sugar

Pour milk into 8x8x2-inch pan; freeze till ice crystals form around edges. Meanwhile, in saucepan combine brown sugar, gelatin, and ¼ teaspoon *salt*. Add pumpkin, egg yolks, cinnamon, nutmeg, ginger, and 1¼ cups *cold water*. Cook and stir over low heat till thickened. Remove from heat; chill till partially set. Beat egg whites to soft peaks. Gradually add granulated sugar, beating to stiff peaks; fold into pumpkin mixture. Whip icy milk to stiff peaks; fold into pumpkin mixture. Turn into 2-quart soufflé dish with foil collar; chill till firm. Makes 12 servings.

Fruit-Sauced Bread Pudding

4 slightly beaten eggs
2 cups *reconstituted* nonfat dry milk *or* milk
¼ cup granulated sugar
½ teaspoon vanilla
½ teaspoon ground cinnamon
4 slices day-old bread, cut into ½-inch cubes
½ cup packed brown sugar
1 tablespoon cornstarch
1 cup chopped peeled apples *or* peaches
3 tablespoons margarine
1 beaten egg
1 teaspoon vanilla

Combine first 5 ingredients and ¼ teaspoon *salt*; stir in bread cubes. Turn into ungreased 8x1½-inch round baking dish. Bake in 325° oven about 45 minutes or till knife inserted near center comes out clean. Meanwhile, prepare sauce. Combine brown sugar, cornstarch, and dash *salt*. Add fruit, margarine, and ½ cup *water*. Cook and stir till bubbly. Gradually stir some of the hot mixture into the 1 beaten egg. Return to saucepan; cook and stir 1 minute more. Add 1 teaspoon vanilla. Spoon sauce over each serving. Serves 6.

Easy Orange Sherbet

This velvety-smooth sherbet is surprisingly easy to make—

1 cup evaporated milk
1 6-ounce can frozen orange juice concentrate, thawed
⅓ cup sugar

Pour evaporated milk into 8x8x2-inch pan; freeze till ice crystals form around edges. In small mixer bowl beat the icy milk with rotary beater or electric mixer till stiff peaks form. Beat in orange juice concentrate and sugar. Return mixture to pan; freeze 1½ to 2 hours or till nearly firm; stir. Freeze till firm. Makes 10 servings.

Easy Snack Cake

Chocolate pudding mix flavors this very moist cake—

1½ cups all-purpose flour
¾ cup granulated sugar
1 4-serving-size package *regular* chocolate pudding mix
1½ teaspoons baking soda
⅓ cup cooking oil
1 tablespoon vinegar
1 teaspoon vanilla
Sifted powdered sugar (optional)

In small mixer bowl stir together flour, granulated sugar, pudding mix, baking soda, and ½ teaspoon *salt*. Add oil, vinegar, vanilla, and 1 cup *water*. Mix at low speed of electric mixer till blended. Beat for 2 minutes at medium speed. Spread batter evenly in greased and lightly floured 9x9x2-inch baking pan. Bake in 350° oven 25 to 30 minutes or till cake tests done. Cool on wire rack. Sprinkle with powdered sugar, if desired. Makes 9 to 12 servings.

Carrot-Banana Cake

- 1¼ cups all-purpose flour
- 1 cup granulated sugar
- 1 teaspoon baking powder
- 1 teaspoon baking soda
- ¾ teaspoon ground cinnamon
- 1 cup finely shredded carrot
- ⅔ cup mashed ripe banana (2 medium)
- ½ cup cooking oil
- 2 eggs
- Sifted powdered sugar

In mixer bowl stir together the flour, granulated sugar, baking powder, soda, cinnamon, and ½ teaspoon *salt*; add carrot, banana, oil, and eggs. Mix at low speed of electric mixer till moistened; beat at medium speed for 2 minutes. Pour into greased and lightly floured 9x9x2-inch baking pan. Bake in 350° oven for 30 to 35 minutes or till wooden pick inserted in center comes out clean. Cool. Sprinkle with powdered sugar, if desired. Makes 9 to 12 servings.

Saucy Pineapple Cake

- 1 15½-ounce can crushed pineapple
- 1 4-serving-size package *regular* vanilla pudding mix
- 1 package 1-layer-size yellow cake mix

In saucepan combine *undrained* pineapple, pudding mix, and ⅓ cup *water*. Cook and stir till thickened and bubbly. Pour into greased 9x9x2-inch baking pan. Prepare cake mix according to package directions; pour batter over pineapple mixture in pan. Bake in 350° oven 30 to 35 minutes or till cake tests done. Cool 10 minutes; invert onto serving plate. Makes 9 to 12 servings.

Creamy Lime Dessert

- 1 4-serving-size package *regular* lemon pudding mix
- 1 3-ounce package lime-flavored gelatin
- 3½ cups cold water
- 2 slightly beaten egg yolks
- 2 egg whites
- 2 tablespoons sugar
- Lemony Whipped Topping (see recipe, page 77)

In saucepan combine lemon pudding mix and lime-flavored gelatin. Gradually stir in *2 cups* of the cold water. Cook and stir till thickened and bubbly. Stir about *1 cup* hot mixture into slightly beaten egg yolks. Return all to saucepan; cook and stir 2 minutes more. Remove from heat; add remaining 1½ cups cold water. Chill till partially set (consistency of unbeaten egg whites), stirring frequently.

In mixer bowl beat egg whites till soft peaks form. Gradually add sugar, beating till stiff peaks form. Fold egg whites into lime mixture. Spoon into 8 sherbet glasses or individual dishes. Chill several hours or overnight. To serve, top with Lemony Whipped Topping, if desired. Serves 8.

Applesauce-Oat Cookies

- 1 cup shortening
- 1 cup packed brown sugar
- ½ cup granulated sugar
- 2 eggs
- 1 teaspoon vanilla
- ¾ cup applesauce
- 1¾ cups all-purpose flour
- 1 teaspoon salt
- 1 teaspoon baking soda
- 1 teaspoon ground cinnamon
- 3 cups rolled oats
- 1 cup raisins (optional)

In mixer bowl cream together shortening, brown sugar, and granulated sugar. Add eggs and vanilla; beat well. Add applesauce; mix well.

In mixing bowl stir together the flour, salt, baking soda, and cinnamon. Add to creamed mixture; stir till well blended. Stir in rolled oats and raisins, if desired. Drop dough from teaspoon onto greased baking sheet. Bake in 375° oven about 12 minutes or till golden brown. Remove from cookie sheet; cool on wire rack. Makes about 5 dozen cookies.

Oatmeal Crinkle Cookies

These chewy sugar-topped oat cookies are ideal for stocking the cookie jar—

- 1 cup all-purpose flour
- ½ cup granulated sugar
- ½ cup packed brown sugar
- ½ teaspoon baking powder
- ½ teaspoon baking soda
- ¼ teaspoon salt
- ½ cup shortening
- 1 egg
- ¼ teaspoon vanilla
- ¾ cup rolled oats
- ¼ cup chopped nuts (optional)
- Granulated sugar

In mixer bowl combine flour, the ½ cup granulated sugar, the brown sugar, baking powder, baking soda, and salt. Add shortening, egg, and vanilla; beat well. Stir in rolled oats and nuts, if desired.

Using a rounded teaspoon for each, shape dough into balls; dip one side of ball in some granulated sugar. Place, sugar side up, on ungreased cookie sheet. Bake in 350° oven for 12 to 15 minutes or till golden brown. Remove from cookie sheet; cool on wire rack. Makes about 3 ½ dozen cookies.

COOKING for FRIENDS

A party is a special time for food and fellowship. On the next seven pages we've spotlighted three types of entertaining when cooking for friends: a special-occasion dinner, brunch, and all-occasion snacks.

Special Occasion

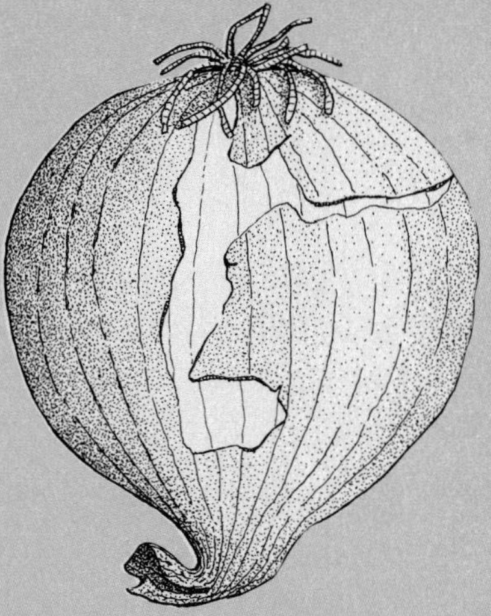

This meal for eight brings elegance to your dining table on any special occasion.

With careful planning and shopping, you'll be able to prepare an impressive and elaborate meal, and still stay within your food budget.

Begin with Appetizer Onion Soup to whet the appetite. Carve Cherry-Glazed Turkey at the table and accompany the entrée with a fruit mold or spinach salad, meringue-topped broccoli spears, a rich pasta toss, and homemade French bread. And for dessert, slice refreshing Sherbet Melba Bombe, an impressive way to end the meal.

Menu

Appetizer Onion Soup
Cherry-Glazed Turkey
Cran-Raspberry and Sour Cream Mold *or* **Vegetable-Spinach Salad**
Snowcapped Broccoli Spears
Parslied Pasta Toss
French Bread
Margarine *or* **Butter**
Sherbet Melba Bombe
Coffee Tea

Appetizer Onion Soup

Good enough to begin any meal—

- 6 medium onions, thinly sliced and separated into rings (3 cups)
- 1/4 cup margarine *or* butter
- 2 10 1/2-ounce cans condensed beef broth
- 2 cups water
- 1 teaspoon worcestershire sauce
- 1/4 teaspoon salt
- 1/8 teaspoon pepper
- 2 French *or* hard rolls, sliced and toasted, *or* 4 slices bread, halved and toasted
- Grated parmesan cheese *or* sliced Swiss *or* other cheese

In large saucepan or Dutch oven cook sliced onions in margarine or butter about 20 minutes or till tender and lightly browned. Stir in beef broth, water, worcestershire sauce, salt, and pepper; bring to boiling. Sprinkle toasted rolls or bread slices with parmesan cheese or place a slice of cheese atop toast. Place under broiler till cheese is lightly browned. Ladle soup into bowls; float toast slices atop. Makes 8 servings.

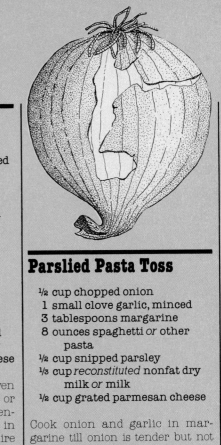

Parslied Pasta Toss

- 1/2 cup chopped onion
- 1 small clove garlic, minced
- 3 tablespoons margarine
- 8 ounces spaghetti *or* other pasta
- 1/2 cup snipped parsley
- 1/3 cup *reconstituted* nonfat dry milk *or* milk
- 1/2 cup grated parmesan cheese

Cook onion and garlic in margarine till onion is tender but not brown. Meanwhile, cook spaghetti or other pasta according to package directions; drain. Toss hot pasta with onion mixture, snipped parsley, milk, and dash *pepper*; add parmesan and toss again. Season to taste. Serve immediately. Makes 8 servings.

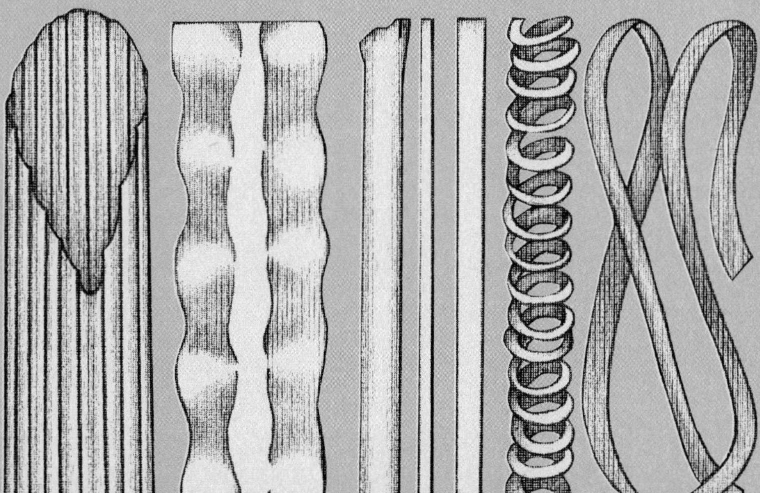

Special Occasion

Cran-Raspberry and Sour Cream Mold

- 2 3-ounce packages *or* one 6-ounce package raspberry-flavored gelatin
- 1¾ cups boiling water
- 1 20-ounce can crushed pineapple
- 1 16-ounce can whole cranberry sauce
- 1 cup dairy sour cream

Dissolve gelatin in the boiling water. Stir in *undrained* pineapple and the cranberry sauce till cranberry sauce melts. Chill till partially set. Pour *half* of the fruit mixture into a 6½-cup ring mold; chill till almost firm (let remaining gelatin stand at room temperature). Stir sour cream; spread evenly over gelatin in mold. Gently spoon remaining gelatin mixture on top of sour cream layer. Chill several hours or overnight till firm. Makes 8 to 10 servings.

French Bread

- 5½ to 6 cups all-purpose flour
- 2 packages active dry yeast;
- 2 cups warm water (115° to 120°)
- Cornmeal

In large mixer bowl combine *2 cups* of the flour, the yeast, and 2 teaspoons *salt*. Add warm water. Beat at low speed of electric mixer for ½ minute, scraping sides of bowl constantly. Beat 3 minutes at high speed. Stir in as much of the remaining flour as you can mix in using a spoon.

Turn dough out onto lightly floured surface. Knead in enough of the remaining flour to make a stiff dough that is smooth and elastic (8 to 10 minutes total). Shape into a ball. Place in lightly greased bowl; turn once to grease surface. Cover; let rise in warm place till double (1 to 1¼ hours).

Punch down; turn out onto lightly floured surface. Divide in half. Cover; let rest 10 minutes. Roll each half into a 15x12-inch rectangle. Roll up tightly from long side; seal. Taper ends. Place, seam side down, on greased baking sheet sprinkled with cornmeal. Cover; let rise till nearly double (about 45 minutes).

With sharp knife, make 3 or 4 diagonal cuts about ¼ inch deep across tops of loaves. Bake in 375° oven for 40 to 45 minutes. Cool on wire rack. Makes 2 loaves.

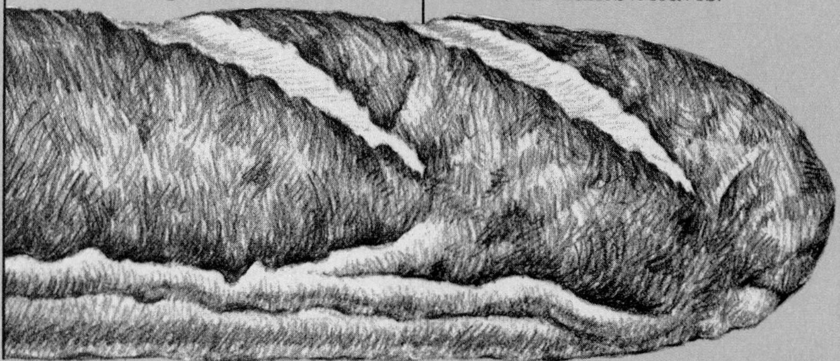

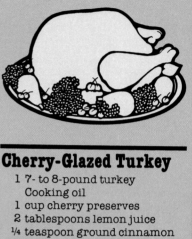

Cherry-Glazed Turkey

- 1 7- to 8-pound turkey
- Cooking oil
- 1 cup cherry preserves
- 2 tablespoons lemon juice
- ¼ teaspoon ground cinnamon
- ¼ teaspoon ground cloves

Place turkey, breast side up, on a rack in shallow roasting pan. Tuck drumsticks under band of skin across tail, or tie legs securely to tail. Twist wing tips under back. Brush turkey with cooking oil. If meat thermometer is used, insert in center of inside thigh muscle making sure bulb does not touch bone. Cover loosely with foil "cap" that barely touches the turkey. Press lightly at ends of drumsticks and neck. Roast in 325° oven for a total of 3½ to 4 hours. Baste dry areas of skin occasionally with pan drippings or cooking oil during roasting.

Meanwhile, for glaze, in saucepan combine cherry preserves, lemon juice, and spices. Cut up any large pieces of cherry. Cook and stir till boiling. Reduce heat; simmer for 1 minute more.

After the turkey has cooked about 2½ hours (or when two-thirds done), cut band of skin or string between legs. About 45 minutes before turkey is done, remove foil. Brush turkey frequently with glaze during last 30 minutes of roasting. Turkey is done when meat thermometer registers 185° and drumstick moves easily in socket. Spoon any remaining glaze over turkey before serving. Makes 8 servings.

Snowcapped Broccoli Spears

This elegant yet easy broccoli side dish is topped with a creamy meringuelike mixture—

- 3 10-ounce packages frozen broccoli spears
- 2 tablespoons margarine *or* butter, melted
- 3 egg whites
- ½ teaspoon salt
- ½ cup salad dressing *or* mayonnaise
- 3 tablespoons grated parmesan cheese

Cook frozen broccoli according to package directions; drain well. Arrange broccoli spears in a 9-inch pie plate with stem ends to the center. Brush broccoli with melted margarine or butter.

In mixer bowl beat egg whites and salt using an electric mixer till stiff peaks form. Gently fold in salad dressing or mayonnaise. Spoon salad dressing-egg white mixture into center of pie plate atop broccoli spears; sprinkle with grated parmesan cheese.

Bake in 350° oven for 12 to 15 minutes or till salad dressing mixture is golden and broccoli is heated through. Makes 8 servings.

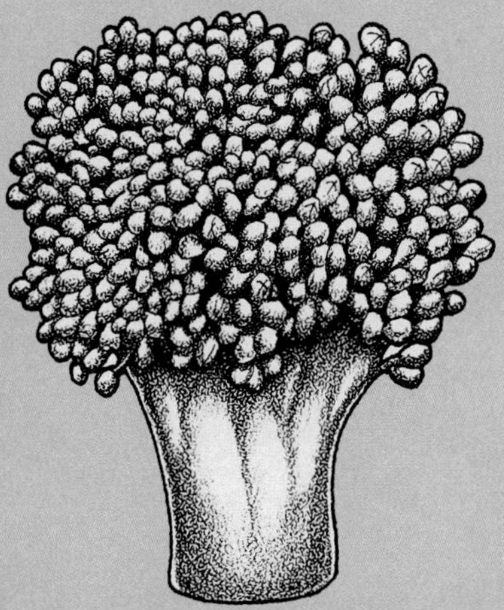

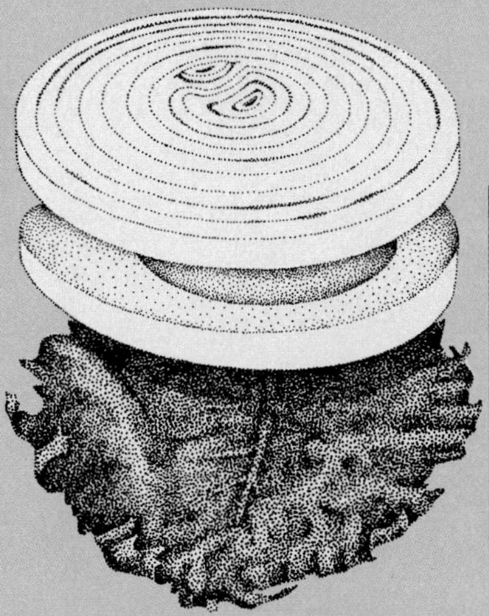

Vegetable-Spinach Salad

- 1 small onion
- ½ cup salad oil
- 3 tablespoons catsup
- 2 tablespoons sugar
- 2 tablespoons vinegar
- 2 teaspoons worcestershire sauce
- 4 slices bacon
- 7 cups torn fresh spinach *or* assorted greens
- ½ of a 16-ounce can bean sprouts, drained, *or* one 8-ounce can water chestnuts, drained and sliced
- 1 medium carrot, thinly bias sliced
- 2 hard-cooked eggs, cut into wedges

Halve onion crosswise; cut up half and slice remaining half. Separate slices into rings and set aside.

For dressing, in blender container combine cut up onion, oil, catsup, sugar, vinegar, worcestershire, ¼ teaspoon *salt*, and dash *pepper*. Cover; blend till smooth. Chill.

Cook bacon till crisp. Drain, crumble, and set aside. Place spinach or assorted greens in salad bowl. Add sprouts or water chestnuts, carrot, onion rings, and bacon; toss. Drizzle desired amount of dressing over salad; top with eggs. Refrigerate remaining dressing. Serves 8.

Sherbet Melba Bombe

- 2 cups plain granola cereal, crushed
- 2 tablespoons margarine *or* butter, melted
- 1 quart lemon sherbet *or* frozen lemon yogurt
- ½ cup seedless raspberry jam
- 1 pint raspberry sherbet *or* frozen raspberry yogurt

Combine granola and melted margarine or butter till blended. Pat about ¼ of mixture into bottom of 6-cup bombe mold or mixing bowl lined with clear plastic wrap. Freeze 10 minutes. Spoon *half* the lemon sherbet or frozen yogurt evenly atop crumbs in mold. Spoon

half the jam on top, spreading to ½ inch of edge. Sprinkle with another ¼ of crumbs. Return to freezer for 20 minutes or till firm.

Spoon the raspberry sherbet or frozen yogurt evenly into mold. Spoon remaining jam atop, spreading to within ½ inch of edge. Sprinkle with another ¼ of the crumbs. If mixture seems soft, return to freezer about 20 minutes. Top with remaining lemon sherbet or frozen yogurt and crumbs. Freeze several hours or till firm. Remove from freezer 10 minutes before serving. Invert onto serving plate; remove plastic wrap. Cut into wedges. Makes 8 servings.

Brunch

Combine breakfast and lunch into one satisfying brunch featuring saucy egg-filled cream puffs, a fruit bowl, warm coffee cake, zesty meatballs, and a selection of beverages.

Menu

Eggs-and-Cheese Cream Puffs
Spiced Fruit Compote
Pumpkin Streusel Coffee Cake
Margarine or Butter
Sausage Brunch Meatballs
Pick-a-Fruit Nog
Spiced Coffee Tea Milk

Eggs-and-Cheese Cream Puffs

Cream Puffs (see recipe, page 82)
6 tablespoons margarine or butter
1/3 cup all-purpose flour
3/4 teaspoon salt
2 3/4 cups *reconstituted* nonfat dry milk *or* milk
1 1/2 cups shredded Swiss cheese *or* process cheese spread (6 ounces)
1/2 cup chopped onion
1/4 cup chopped green pepper
3 tablespoons margarine *or* butter, melted
12 beaten eggs
1/3 cup *reconstituted* nonfat dry milk *or* milk
Paprika (optional)

Prepare Cream Puffs as directed *except* do not fill with suggested dessert fillings. Set aside.

In saucepan melt the 6 tablespoons margarine or butter. Blend in flour, salt, and 1/8 teaspoon *pepper*. Add the 2 3/4 cups milk all at once. Cook and stir till thickened and bubbly. Remove *1 cup* of the white sauce; set aside. Add shredded Swiss cheese or process cheese spread to remaining sauce mixture; stir to melt. Keep cheese sauce warm while preparing eggs.

In skillet cook onion and green pepper in the 3 tablespoons margarine or butter till vegetables are tender but not brown. Meanwhile, combine eggs with the 1/3 cup milk. Pour into skillet with vegetables. Cook, without stirring, till mixture starts to set on bottom and sides. Lift and fold the partially cooked eggs so the uncooked portion flows underneath. Continue cooking eggs about 2 minutes or till partially set. Add the reserved 1 cup white sauce; stir gently to combine. Continue cooking egg mixture for 3 to 5 minutes more or till egg mixture is set throughout but still moist and creamy. Remove from heat. Spoon about *1/2 cup* egg mixture into each cooled cream puff. Replace tops. Drizzle filled cream puffs with some of the cheese sauce; sprinkle with paprika, if desired. Pass remaining sauce. Serves 10.

Spiced Fruit Compote

1 20-ounce can pineapple chunks
2 tablespoons lemon juice
1 teaspoon finely shredded orange peel
1/2 teaspoon ground cinnamon
4 oranges
4 apples, cored and cut into bite-size pieces
3 bananas, sliced
1 16-ounce package frozen whole unsweetened strawberries, thawed, *or* 3 cups fresh strawberries

Drain pineapple, reserving liquid; set pineapple chunks aside. Combine pineapple liquid, lemon juice, orange peel, and cinnamon. Peel and section oranges over bowl, reserving juice. Add orange juice to spiced pineapple liquid.

In large bowl combine pineapple chunks, orange sections, apple pieces, sliced bananas, and strawberries. Add spiced pineapple juice mixture to assorted fruit mixture; stir gently to combine. Chill before serving. Makes 10 servings.

Pumpkin-Streusel Coffee Cake

Use leftover canned pumpkin to make Pumpkin Dessert Soufflé on page 82—

- 1 cup granulated sugar
- ¼ cup margarine *or* butter
- 2 eggs
- 1 teaspoon vanilla
- 2 cups all-purpose flour
- 1 tablespoon baking powder
- ½ teaspoon salt
- ¾ cup *reconstituted* nonfat dry milk *or* milk
- ½ cup canned pumpkin
- ⅓ cup all-purpose flour
- ¼ cup packed brown sugar
- 1 teaspoon ground cinnamon
- 2 tablespoons margarine *or* butter

In mixer bowl cream together granulated sugar and the ¼ cup margarine or butter. Beat in eggs and vanilla.

Stir together the 2 cups flour, the baking powder, and salt; add to creamed mixture alternately with milk. Blend the pumpkin with ¾ *cup* of the batter. Spread remaining batter in a greased 8x8x2-inch baking pan. Drop pumpkin mixture over batter by teaspoonfuls.

Combine ⅓ cup flour, the brown sugar, and cinnamon; cut in 2 tablespoons margarine or butter. Sprinkle over coffee cake. Bake in 350° oven 40 to 45 minutes. Serve warm. Makes 8 to 10 servings.

Sausage Brunch Meatballs

- 2 beaten eggs
- ¼ cup *reconstituted* nonfat dry milk *or* milk
- ½ cup fine dry bread crumbs (2 slices)
- ⅓ cup finely chopped onion
- 3 tablespoons snipped parsley (optional)
- 1 tablespoon worcestershire sauce
- ¾ teaspoon salt
- 1 pound bulk pork sausage
- ½ pound ground pork *or* ground beef
- ½ cup apricot, peach, *or* pineapple preserves
- ⅓ cup bottled barbecue sauce
- 3 tablespoons water

In mixing bowl combine eggs and milk; stir in dry bread crumbs, chopped onion, snipped parsley, worcestershire sauce, and salt. Add sausage and ground pork or ground beef; mix well.

Shape meat mixture into 1-inch meatballs. Place in 15x10x1-inch baking pan. Bake in 350° oven for 25 to 30 minutes or till done.

Meanwhile, prepare sauce. In small saucepan combine choice of preserves, barbecue sauce, and water. Heat through. Drain fat off meatballs. Transfer meatballs to serving dish; keep warm. Pour hot sauce over meatballs. Serve meatballs warm with wooden picks. Makes 8 to 10 servings.

Pick-a-Fruit Nog

- 2 8-ounce cartons blueberry, strawberry, orange, *or* peach yogurt
- 2 cups *reconstituted* nonfat dry milk *or* milk
- 2 cups fresh *or* frozen unsweetened blueberries, strawberries, orange sections, *or* peaches
- 2 eggs
- ½ teaspoon vanilla
- 4 to 6 ice cubes

In blender container place *half* of the following: the yogurt, milk, fruit, eggs, and vanilla. Cover; blend at high speed till frothy.

Add *half* the ice cubes, one at a time, through hole in lid of blender or with lid ajar, blending till smooth after each addition. Pour into glasses. Repeat with remaining ingredients. Makes 8 servings.

Spiced Coffee

- ⅓ cup packed brown sugar
- ⅓ cup instant coffee crystals
- ½ teaspoon ground nutmeg
- 8 cups *reconstituted* nonfat dry milk *or* milk

In saucepan combine brown sugar, coffee crystals, nutmeg, and dash *salt*. Stir in milk till blended. Heat through but *do not boil*. Serve in mugs. Makes 8 cups.

Snacks

Give a new excitement to snacking. These tempting snacks combine fun, extraordinary treats, and good, wholesome eating. Whatever the reason, a patio party, appetizer party, after-the-ball-game gathering, or just after-school nibbles, make snacking an all-occasion affair.

Menu

Fruity Yogurt Kabobs
Whole Wheat Crackers
Fifty-Fifty Dip
Sweet-Sour Frank Appetizers *or* **Hot Cheese Dunk**
Assorted Crisp Vegetable Dippers and Bread Cubes
Mulled Beverage Mix
Orange Jupiter
Herbed Spinach Snack Balls

Fruity Yogurt Kabobs

1 8¼-ounce can pineapple chunks
2 medium apples
2 medium bananas
1 8-ounce carton plain *or* fruit-flavored yogurt
Flaked coconut, toasted, *or* granola

Drain pineapple, reserving syrup. Core apples; cut into bite-size pieces. Slice bananas into ½-inch pieces. Dip apple and banana pieces into reserved pineapple syrup. Using 4- to 5-inch long cocktail skewers, alternately skewer apple pieces, banana slices, and pineapple chunks.

Spread with plain or flavored yogurt; sprinkle with coconut or granola. (Or, if using wooden picks, individually skewer a piece of fruit, dip in yogurt, and roll in coconut or granola.) Makes about 18.

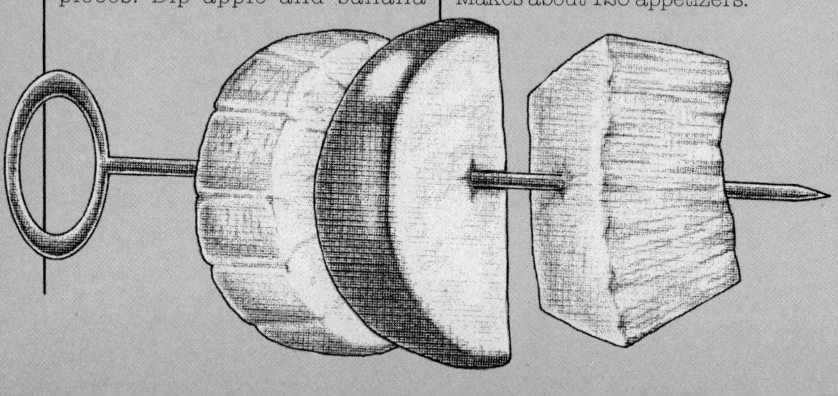

Sweet-Sour Frank Appetizers

1 15½-ounce can pineapple chunks
2 tablespoons cornstarch
¼ teaspoon salt
⅓ cup maple-flavored syrup
¼ cup vinegar
1 pound frankfurters, cut into ¾-inch pieces
1 medium green pepper, cut into ¾-inch squares

Drain pineapple chunks, reserving syrup. Add enough water to syrup to equal 1 cup. In large skillet blend pineapple syrup mixture into cornstarch and salt; stir in the maple-flavored syrup and vinegar. Cook and stir till thickened and bubbly. Add pineapple chunks, frankfurters, and green pepper; heat through.

Turn frankfurter mixture into serving dish; keep warm. (Or, turn mixture into blazer pan of chafing dish. Keep warm over hot water.) Serve warm with wooden picks. Makes about 120 appetizers.

Whole Wheat Crackers

1 cup whole wheat flour
1 cup all-purpose flour
⅓ cup sugar
2 teaspoons baking powder
1 teaspoon baking soda
½ teaspoon salt
½ teaspoon cream of tartar
½ cup margarine *or* butter
¾ cup buttermilk *or* sour milk (See tip, page 72)

In mixing bowl stir together dry ingredients; cut in margarine or butter till mixture resembles coarse crumbs. Add buttermilk or sour milk all at once. Stir with fork just till dough follows fork around bowl.

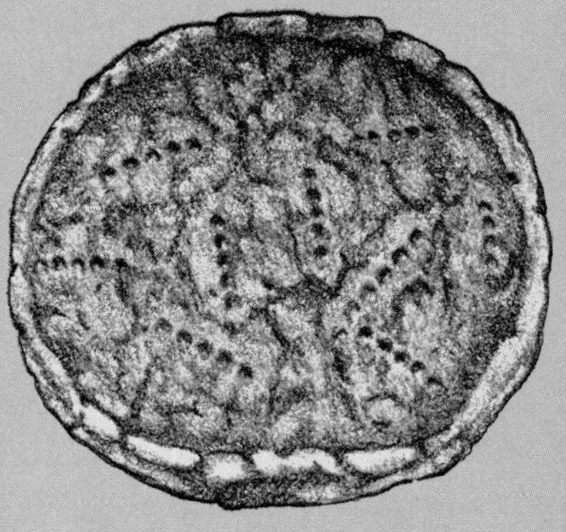

On floured surface roll out dough to *¼-inch* thickness. Cut with floured 2½-inch biscuit cutter to make about 2 dozen biscuits. Place on baking sheet. Bake in 350° oven 12 to 15 minutes or till lightly browned. Split hot biscuits with sharp knife; place, cut side up, on baking sheet. Dry in 300° oven 15 to 20 minutes. Makes 4 dozen crackers.

For thinner crackers, stir together ingredients as directed. Roll out on floured surface to *1/16-inch* thickness. Cut with floured 2½-inch biscuit cutter. Prick with fork. Place on ungreased baking sheet; bake in 350° oven 12 to 15 minutes or till lightly browned. Makes 6 to 8 dozen crackers.

Fifty-Fifty Dip

1 cup cream-style cottage cheese
½ of a 0.6- or 0.7-ounce package green goddess, blue cheese, *or* Italian salad dressing mix
2 teaspoons lemon juice
1 cup plain yogurt
Paprika
Assorted vegetable dippers

Put cottage cheese, salad dressing mix, and lemon juice in blender container. Cover and blend till smooth. Turn into bowl; stir in yogurt. Cover; chill. Sprinkle paprika atop and serve with vegetable dippers. Makes 2 cups.

Hot Cheese Dunk

½ cup nonfat dry milk *powder*
½ cup finely chopped onion
1 small clove garlic, minced
3 tablespoons margarine
3 tablespoons all-purpose flour
2 teaspoons instant chicken bouillon granules
Few drops bottled hot pepper sauce
1½ cups shredded Swiss *or* American cheese *or* process cheese spread
⅓ cup grated parmesan cheese
Reconstituted nonfat dry milk *or* milk
Assorted vegetable dippers *or* bread cubes

Combine milk powder and 1¼ cups *water*; mix well. Set aside. Cook onion and garlic in margarine till tender. Blend in flour and bouillon granules. Add milk mixture and pepper sauce all at once. Cook and stir till thickened. Add cheeses, stirring to melt. Pour into fondue pot or 1-quart casserole; keep warm. Spear dipper with fork; dip into cheese mixture. Serves 8 to 10.

Mulled Beverage Mix

1½ cups water
¾ cup sugar
6 inches stick cinnamon, broken
6 whole cloves
Peel of ¼ lemon, cut into thin strips
½ cup lemon juice
Chilled *or* heated apple juice, cranberry juice cocktail, dry red *or* white wine, rosé wine, *or* sparkling pink catawba grape juice

In saucepan combine water, sugar, cinnamon, cloves, and lemon peel. Bring mixture to boiling, stirring till sugar is dissolved. Reduce heat; cover and simmer for 10 minutes. Stir in lemon juice. Strain mixture through double-thickness cheesecloth. Cover tightly and refrigerate for as long as 6 weeks.

To serve, pour mix into glass or mug; add desired chilled or heated beverage. Use 2 tablespoons mix to ¾ cup (6 ounces) beverage. (Serve chilled drink with ice, if desired.) Garnish each drink with lemon or orange slices and maraschino cherries on a skewer, if desired. Makes 1½ cups mix or enough for 12 servings.

Orange Jupiter

1 cup *reconstituted* nonfat dry milk *or* milk
1 6-ounce can (¾ cup) frozen orange juice concentrate
1 teaspoon vanilla
¼ cup sugar
6 large ice cubes (1½ cups)

In blender container combine milk, orange juice concentrate, vanilla, sugar, and 1 cup cold *water*. Add ice cubes. Cover; blend about 30 seconds or till smooth. Serve at once. Makes 4 to 6 servings.

Herbed Spinach Snack Balls

1 10-ounce package frozen chopped spinach
1½ cups fine dry bread crumbs
½ cup grated parmesan cheese
1 teaspoon poultry seasoning
⅛ teaspoon garlic powder
3 beaten eggs
6 tablespoons margarine *or* butter, melted
Cooking oil *or* shortening for deep-fat frying

Cook spinach according to package directions; drain well. Press spinach to remove excess moisture. Combine spinach, bread crumbs, parmesan, poultry seasoning, garlic powder, and ⅛ teaspoon *pepper*. Combine eggs and melted margarine; add to spinach mixture. Mix well; shape into 1-inch balls. Fry in deep hot fat (365°) for 1 to 2 minutes. (If desired, place balls on baking sheet; freeze firm. Store in moisture-vaporproof container. To use, deep-fat fry at 365° 2 to 3 minutes.) Makes 48.

Index

A-B

C

D-K

L-P

Index

Q-S

T-Z

Leftover Meats

Tips

Fruits & Vegetables Chart

Fruits	Plentiful or Near Peak	Vegetables	Plentiful or Near Peak
Apples	October through December	Beets	June through September
Apricots	June and July	Broccoli	November through March
Cantaloupe	June through September	Cauliflower	October and November
Cherries	June and July	Celery	October through June
Cranberries	October through December	Corn	June through September
Grapefruit	January through April	Cucumbers	May through August
Grapes	August through November	Green beans	May through August
Lemons	June and July	Mushrooms	November through January
Oranges	December through May	Peppers, green	June through August
Peaches	June through September	Sweet potatoes	October through December
Pears	August through November	Radishes	March through May
Rhubarb	February through June	Rutabagas, Turnips	November through January
Strawberries	April through June	Spinach	March and April
Tangerines	November through January	Squash, summer	June through August
Watermelons	May through August	Squash, winter	September through November
Bananas, cabbage, carrots, onions, lettuce, and potatoes are in good supply year round and available in most markets.		Tomatoes	May through August

Sources: U.S. Department of Agriculture; United Fresh Fruit and Vegetable Association